UX Titans

Insights from the world of UX thought leaders

Dr. Benjamin Franz
Dr. Michaela Kauer-Franz

UX Titans: Insights from the World of UX Thought Leaders

Written by Dr. Benjamin Franz & Dr. Michaela Kauer-Franz

Early Buyer Edition V2: July, 2025

ISBN: 978-3-00-081819-6 (print)
ISBN: 978-3-00-081820-2 (ebook)

Publisher:
This book is self-published. More information can be found here: www.uxtitans.com

Table of Content

Welcome to the minds of our UX Titans

What does it mean to work in UX? How can you craft experiences that truly resonate with users? What challenges and rewards define this unique field? And: Is this probably a field you would enjoy working in? This book invites you to explore these questions and more through the collective wisdom of nineteen influential UX professionals – our UX Titans.

Each Titan generously shared their insights, answering the same set of questions. How did they start in UX? What secret tips shaped their success? What skills and mindsets do they see as essential for the future? Their candid responses, sprinkled throughout the chapters, offer a roadmap to navigate the ever-evolving world of UX.

But this book isn't about becoming a Titan. It's about finding your path in UX. There's no single formula for success here – no checklist that guarantees greatness. Instead, this book provides a rich tapestry of perspectives, offering inspiration, tools, and guidance to help you determine if UX is your calling and how to make your mark.

Throughout the book, you'll find reflections from Titans on empathy, perseverance, collaboration, and continuous learning. You'll discover what motivates them, what they've learned from mistakes, and what they believe the future of UX holds. You'll even uncover some of their secret tips – truths that might change how you approach your work or career.

We are incredibly grateful to these nineteen professionals for sharing their journeys, challenges, and wisdom. Their words breathe authenticity into every chapter, bringing a depth of experience that can't be found in a single voice.

Whether you're new to UX, curious about the field, or already working within it, we hope this book offers you something meaningful. Perhaps it will ignite a passion, answer questions, or remind you why UX matters.

So, are you ready to dive into the minds of our Titans and discover what UX might mean for you?

Ben & Michaela

https://www.linkedin.com/in/dr-benjamin-franz/

https://www.linkedin.com/in/dr-michaela-kauer-franz/

How this book was written & how to read it

The journey to create UX Titans began with a simple question: What challenges define the UX field, and how can we share them to help others? As founders of Custom Interactions, a UX agency, we've worked with diverse teams – from Lufthansa pilots to Livanova heart-lung machine operators – and noticed recurring struggles UXers face. We became curious: Were these issues universal? And how were others solving them?

Initially, we asked UXers about their experiences whenever we had the chance. However, the idea for a book took shape after discovering Timothy Ferriss's *Tools of Titans*, which interviews high achievers to uncover their strategies. We focused on influential UXers – our "UX Titans" – using a semi-structured interview format to explore their journeys and wisdom.

Over a year (late 2023 to mid 2024), we conducted 19 interviews, totaling 34 hours. These were transcribed into 520 pages of raw text, then distilled into 342 pages of core insights.

From there, we wrote the book, weaving the Titans' voices into a cohesive whole by quoting them as much as possible.

Selecting our Titans was an exciting step. We set clear criteria to ensure a strong foundation: industry professionals needed a transformational role in companies with over 1,000 employees or to have consulted on products used by millions; academics needed research cited by over 1,000 peers; and public figures needed a UX-focused audience of at least 1,000 followers (for more information on the rules, see Chapter 18). We started with our EU-based network and expanded outward, although connecting with new contacts wasn't always easy. The resulting list of UX Titans is impressive, but not set in stone. We would love to include more insights from a more diverse set of UX Titans in future book editions. Therefore, we added a "Suggest-a-Titan" section on www.uxtitans.com. Feel free to suggest your Titans (or yourself ;-)).

Writing UX Titans has been a journey of discovery, and we're grateful to the Titans and our community for making it possible. We hope it inspires you as much as it has inspired us.

How to read this book:

The book is made to be explored. Every chapter includes a "What to expect," the main interview part, a summary, and a reflective "Our thoughts" section. Our advice:

- **Start with the table of contents**, pick the chapters that interest you most, and dive in.
- **If you are looking for the essentials**, concentrate on the summary and our thoughts.
- **If you are eager to dive into more details**, read the full chapter.

Exclusive Early Buyer Edition: Unlock Your Bonuses

Thank you for joining us on this journey with the *Early Buyer Edition* of UX Titans: Insights from the World of UX Thought Leaders! As a special thank you, we've created exclusive downloadable content to help you apply the Titans' wisdom to your UX career and projects. These resources are designed to give you a head start, whether hiring, advocating for UX, or starting fresh in the field.

Here's what you'll get:

- **Questions for a UX job interview:** Find the perfect UXer for your team with this curated list of questions, or prepare for your job interview.
- **Metrics to showcase UX Return on Investment (ROI):** Demonstrate UX's value with this guide to key metrics. Find the right metric for your product to make a compelling case for UX investment to stakeholders.
- **Cheat Sheet for starting UX in your company:** Introduce UX practices with this step-by-step guide. It's perfect for beginners or teams building a UX culture.

How to Access Your Bonuses

Visit www.uxtitans.com/early-buyer-edition and register to download your exclusive content. These resources are available only to early buyers, so don't miss out!

We can't wait to see how these tools help you grow as a UXer.

Thank you, UX Titans!

Before getting to know the Titans, we would like to take a moment to thank them. When we reached out to them, asking for their insights, we anticipated thoughtful responses, but what we received exceeded our expectations. Every Titan set aside at least two hours to participate in deep conversations, providing candid reflections on their careers, philosophies, and experiences.

Yet their contributions didn't stop there. Many went the extra mile – reviewing drafts, providing feedback, and ensuring that the nuances of their stories and insights were captured authentically.

To all Titans who so graciously contributed to this book: thank you. Thank you for your time, insights, and trust in this project. Thank you for opening up about your struggles and successes and allowing us to share your stories with the world. Your contributions made this book possible.

1

Journeys into UX: From which backgrounds did our Titans come to their profession, and why did they stay there?

Chapter one

Journeys into UX: From which backgrounds did our Titans come to their profession, and why did they stay there?

1.1 What to expect from this chapter

In this chapter, we look into the diverse academic paths taken by our UX Titans, exploring how their various backgrounds have shaped their careers in UX. You will discover how the diverse backgrounds contributed to each Titan's journey and how it ultimately led them to stay in the field for decades. This chapter also highlights the unexpected twists and turns that led our UX Titans to discover their passion for User Experience. You'll learn about the pivotal moments that made them fall in love with the field, often by chance. These stories remind us that sometimes, the most fulfilling paths are those we stumble upon rather than those we meticulously plan.

One word upfront before we start: Each Titan will be heard throughout the book. We will introduce each Titan in more detail when they are cited for the first time. If you want to read more about the Titans upfront: Feel free to look at our last chapter, which gives you a lot more detail on our Titans and how they were selected.

1.2 These are the roads taken: The various backgrounds of our UX Titans.

And now, we explore the diverse backgrounds of our UX Titans, revealing the varied paths that have led them to excel in the field of UX.

- **Psychology:** Psychology is the most common background, with eight experts leveraging their understanding of human behavior and perception in UX design. Those experts are: Bill Albert, Carmen Fehrenbach, Guido Meier-Ahrendt, Kerstin Dyck, Kevin Liang, Marc Hassenzahl, Sarah Diefenbach, and Thomas Vöhringer-Kuhnt.
- **Design:** Three experts, Gert-Dieter Tuzar, Tobias Oberpaul, and Ulf Schubert, transitioned from design to UX, focusing on human-machine interaction and strategic design.
- **Engineering:** Lutz Krauß and Oliver Kulpi demonstrate how engineering skills contribute to UX through system architecture and technical problem-solving.
- **IT/Programming:** Two of our experts (Dominique Winter and Uwe Betzin) use their programming and software

development knowledge to ensure the functionality of UX designs.

- **Natural Sciences:** One UX Titan is a physicist. Nis Boy Naeve applies his analytical skills to solve complex UX problems.
- **Other Backgrounds:** UX also attracts career changers from fields like the military (Matthias Schulz, who learned as a Sports teacher and later studied economic psychology) and photography (Katja Busch), showing the field's versatility and openness to diverse skill sets.

1.3 Digging deeper: What else lured our UX Titans into the field?

We now know what backgrounds our Titans have. But let's dig a little deeper into some stories:

A common thread among many of our UX Titans is a deep passion for designing great products. Almost all our Titans mentioned this underlying passion. We let Dominique Winter[1] speak on behalf of these Titans. Dominique's holistic approach to mastering UX comes from his unwavering commitment to creating and refining products, a love that has continuously shaped his career. He believes that "UX can only be understood holistically and can only be mastered holistically as the task of creating a good user experience." This perspective drives him to stay rooted in the field, continually evolving his role while focusing on helping organizations develop exceptional products and, most of all, improving people's lives by giving them an exceptional experience.

[1] Dominique Winter is a UX expert who helps organizations enhance product development through user-centered design. With experience at OBI Group Holding and REWE Digital, he guides teams in creating impactful, user-driven experiences and shares his knowledge through workshops, talks and podcasts.

For several Titans, including Lutz Krauß, Carmen Fehrenbach, and Kevin Liang, the dynamic and varied nature of UX was a significant draw. Their initial interest was sparked through part-time jobs, internships, or academic theses, highlighting the diversity of UX tasks – a stark contrast to repetitive work. Lutz Krauß[2], for example, transitioned from a monotonous job to the excitement and variety offered by the UX field. Reflecting on his past (before entering Porsche AG), Lutz describes the turning point: "It was coming into the office in the morning, headphones on, sitting in front of the computer, pushing things back and forth. And I thought to myself: 'No, you can't do that. And how will you put up with that for a lifetime?' And then I got to know this human-machine interaction topic." This realization was the catalyst that led Lutz to pursue a career in UX, where every day brings new challenges and opportunities.

[2] Dr. Lutz W.H. Krauß is a seasoned UX expert with over two decades of experience at Porsche AG, where he led key initiatives in app development, Human-Machine Interaction (HMI), and UI/UX design. His roles included heading UI/UX Display and Operation, as well as serving as Internal Customer Success Lead, ensuring the alignment of internal teams, stakeholders, and end-users. Lutz's innovative approach to user-centered design and his leadership in integrating all customer groups into the development process solidify his reputation as a true Titan in the field of UX.

Dominique Winter's enthusiasm for UX is also closely tied to his love for diverse experiences, both personally and professionally. His curiosity drives him to explore new activities, mirroring his approach to UX. Dominique shares, "In my private life, I'm all about experiences. I have learned the craziest things or tried them out just because I wanted to [...] Somehow, I can also make jam. As dull as that sometimes sounds. I still have a motorboat license on my bucket list because it's cool. In the meantime, I like to go ultra-hiking." His passion for life and learning translates seamlessly into his work, where he continuously seeks new challenges and experiences. Dominique also reflects on the fact that he found motivation in realizing that "the task of creating a good user experience" was his true calling, even as his role evolved: "And I quickly realized that I wanted to stay there. My role changes over time. But the topic of wanting to develop great products and helping organizations to develop great products hasn't changed."

On the other hand, Katja Busch's[3] journey into UX was significantly influenced by her background in photography and her curiosity about how aesthetics and advertising affect the brain. Katja's unique path into UX was shaped by her early career in advertising and industrial photography, which instilled in her a deep passion for beautiful design in business contexts. She emphasizes the importance of functionality and usability. As Katja explains, "I have filled many of these UX roles myself: Concept, Information Architecture, Content, Writing, Research, Project Management – interestingly enough, except for UI or Visual Design. My first professional step after school was to train as a photographer. So, I have this basic enthusiasm and feeling for beautiful aesthetics, but for me, it must also work outside of pure art and fulfill its purpose for the client."

[3] Katja Busch is UX coach, consultant, project manager, trainer and speaker. Coming from the field of photography she combines the appreciation of aesthetics with a focus on functionality. Over the last 20 years, she leveraged this background in diverse projects as freelance UX professional for big and small companies.

1.4 Digging deeper, part 2 - It wasn't the plan, but it was love at first sight.

While digging deeper, we realized something: none of our Titans initially set out to pursue UX. Instead, they discovered the field through various serendipitous experiences, including chance lectures, mentors, internships, and part-time jobs. Their journey into UX was often driven by a desire to find better solutions and enhance their work. This might be, to some degree, due to the fact that UX was not as big as it is today when they started in the field. You could even say some of our Titans contributed in a way that led the field to where it is today: Offering direct pathways to UX by providing UX studies at multiple universities. But let's look more closely at how our Titans got where they are now.

Bill Albert[4], for instance, stumbled into UX while researching attention navigation systems. His focus on designing technology that minimizes user distraction led him to a broader exploration of human factors. He reflects, "That opened the door for me to think more about human factors [...] I had to decide which direction to go, and I stumbled upon it."

[4] Dr. Bill Albert is a trailblazer in UX, renowned for his leadership in validating product desirability and achieving product-market fit through innovative methodologies at Greenlight Idea Lab. With key roles at Bentley University, Mach49, and Fidelity Investments, he has transformed UX practices globally, integrating AI, mentoring teams, and driving impactful solutions. As a prolific author and thought leader, his work continues to shape the UX industry, solidifying his legacy as a visionary in the field.

Uwe Betzin's[5] entry into UX was similarly lucky. Driven by frustration with his UI designs, he discovered UX tools through an internal training course at SAP. Uwe describes his revelation: "I went out and said: 'This is how I want to work – there is no other way.'"

[5] Uwe Betzin is an influential UX leader with over 20 years of experience in software development and design. As the Head of UX at generic.de, he integrates Dual Track Agile and Clean Code Development to create intuitive, user-centered enterprise software. With a background, spanning roles from senior developer to UX expert at SAP, Uwe has shaped innovative products like S/4HANA and trained thousands through his "Design Eye Opener" course. His holistic approach to software development and his commitment to fostering a UX mindset across teams make him a true Titan in the UX field.

Carmen Fehrenbach's[6] turning point came through an internship at SAP, where she instantly realized that usability was her true path. She says, "I got into the subject through a part-time job, an internship at SAP. And then, I knew that usability was what I wanted to do."

[6] Carmen Fehrenbach, Manager of UX at Deutsche Telekom, is a highly accomplished expert in user-centered design with over 20 years of experience. Her career includes roles at SAP, User Interface Design GmbH, and SapientNitro, where she developed expertise in interaction design, usability testing, and prototyping. As a certified Design Thinking Facilitator and Systemic Counsellor, Carmen blends technical skill with empathetic strategies to create innovative digital experiences. With 11+ years at Deutsche Telekom, she has led impactful UX projects, earning her recognition as a leader shaping the future of user experience design. In recent years she has also taken on the role of Epic Owner Accessibility, focusing on people with impairments.

Kevin Liang[7] faced initial doubts about his fit in the tech industry due to his psychology background. However, discovering UX illuminated how his skills could bridge his interests with the tech world. He notes, "I thought, 'Oh, a tech company is only for software engineers. What could someone with my background do in a tech company?' UX came to me in a way that showed me my path."

[7] Kevin Liang is a UX researcher and educator with over 14 years of experience across Fortune 500 companies and startups. A passionate mentor, he founded the Zero to UX Research Masterclass, training aspiring UX researchers in both technical and leadership skills. Kevin has co-invented patents, launched over 100 software and hardware products, and played a key role in pioneering research methods, including for Android Wear and autonomous vehicles at Volkswagen. His YouTube channel, where he shares insights and resources on UX research, has garnered over 28,000 subscribers. With a unique blend of experience, creativity, and a dedication to mentorship, Kevin is a leading figure in the UX field.

Gabriela Gomes[8] reflects on her journey: "Creating bits and pieces into a cohesive experience [...] I realized I like the technology and digital media part of it. After that, I went to do a master's in interactive media and game design."

[8] Gabriela Purri R. Gomes is an award-winning UX designer with over 10 years of experience, specializing in human-centered design, inclusive innovation, and immersive technologies. Her work spans industries like digital tech, telecommunications, healthcare, and entertainment, where she leads digital product development and R&D. Recognized internationally, Gabriela's contributions focus on creating accessible, impactful solutions that prioritize human diversity and experience. She has held influential roles at Deutsche Telekom and USC, shaping the future of UX through strategic leadership and cutting-edge innovation.

All of our Titans met UX for the first time and fell in love immediately. Each and every one of our Titans stressed how improving products and working in a different way resonated deeply with them from the beginning. But passion can change over time, so what made them stay in the field for decades?

1.5 What made our UX Titans stay in the field?

Many of our nineteen UX Titans experienced pivotal moments that solidified their decision to remain in the field. One key factor was the dynamic nature of UX, which, as Kevin Liang put it, "never gets old," offering constant variety and challenges.

Early successes also played a crucial role in the journey of our Titans. For example, Nis Boy Naeve[9] discovered his passion during a program at SAP, realizing that "many people were listening to us."

[9] Nis Boy Naeve is a UX Titan with nearly 30 years of experience at SAP AG, where he served as Chief Product Officer and Vice President. He has played a key role in defining and implementing SAP's UI strategy, leading initiatives in UI governance, and developing key UI frameworks. His work, guided by lean principles and a focus on user productivity, has had a lasting impact on SAP's UX evolution and the broader enterprise software landscape, solidifying his status as a leader in the field.

Oliver Kulpi[10] was hooked after developing a pioneering digital tool, recounting, "And when my fellow student and I installed a plug-in in Netscape... I said: 'Martin, that's the future, we have to do something about it.'"

[10] Oliver Kulpi is co-CEO of Digital Experiences Group and is Managing Director at Ergosign GmbH (a German-based UX Design Agency). He has extensive experience designing leadership and strategic roles across various organizations, including Valtech and Publicis Sapient.

The intellectual challenge and discovery within UX captivated many Titans. Gert-Dieter Tuzar[11] was drawn in by the field's "newness and complexity," explaining that he wanted to continue in UX because it was "clear to me that this area challenged me intellectually."

[11] Gert-Dieter Tuzar is a Senior Expert in UX and HMI with over 25 years of experience, having worked at leading companies like Faurecia, Visteon Electronics, and Johnson Controls Automotive. With a Master's in Design Development from The Ohio State University and a background in Industrial Design, he specializes in creating innovative, user-centered interfaces for complex systems, particularly in the automotive sector. Tuzar's expertise in blending human-centered design with advanced technology has made him a recognized leader in UX and HMI.

Similarly, Kerstin Dyck[12] found excitement in the then-new regulatory requirements for medical usability, noting, "I immediately found it very exciting to make a user-centered design process mandatory and got stuck in."

[12] Kerstin Dyck is UX Lead at BTP Design, SAP, with more than 17 years of experience in UX. With a strong background in psychology, user research is an important part of her work in user experience and service design to create sustainable, user-centered solutions. Her past and current leadership roles, including managing teams and budgets, showcase her ability to drive innovation and strategy across projects. Her dedication to sustainability and meaningful design makes her a standout figure in the UX field.

Guido Meier-Arendt[13] was inspired by the joy of solving fundamental UX questions, such as, "How do I measure perceptibility?".

[13] Guido Meier-Arendt is a renowned expert in Human-Machine Interaction (HMI), previously serving as an HMI Expert at Continental AG. With over two decades of experience, his work focuses on user-centered design for automotive technologies, particularly in the fields of advanced driver assistance systems (ADAS) and automated driving. Guido's research on adaptive, multimodal interfaces has significantly influenced the development of safer and more intuitive vehicle interfaces, solidifying his position as a leading figure in the UX field. His contributions continue to shape both academic and industry standards for user experience in automotive HMI design.

The opportunity to design for real impact was another powerful motivator. Titans like Katja Busch were driven by the excitement of creating technology that genuinely helps users, recalling a moment of interaction that made her think, "We can make the information space more compact and completely new."

Ulf Schubert[14] had a moment of revelation about the value of good UX, stating, "I studied media design and then had a triggering moment during my studies. I started working a lot with 3D graphics or 3D animations and then spent weeks and months learning this program called Alias Wavefront. It has a manual that weighs about five kilos, and it takes months to get through it and understand what it does. And it takes even longer before you can do good things with it, and then suddenly, during my studies, the software Maya came along and turned modeling on its head. And suddenly, things that had previously been difficult were straightforward. And that was this moment for me: Wait, why is that?"

[14] Ulf Schubert is a highly experienced UX and CX leader with over 20 years of expertise in the B2B software industry, specializing in user-centered design, customer experience, and strategic management. Currently serving as Director of UX & Touchpoint Design at DATEV eG, he excels in helping organizations develop award-winning digital products and customer experiences. Ulf is passionate about empowering businesses to leverage data-driven insights, build agile teams, and drive organizational change. He also mentors UX professionals and leads the Experience Leadership Club, promoting knowledge-sharing and leadership development. His multifaceted expertise and leadership have made him a Titan in the field of UX and CX.

The field also allowed some Titans to combine their passions; Gabriela Gomes, for example, appreciated how UX allowed her to explore various areas, saying, "With user experience, you can explore many areas in one lifetime."

Carmen Fehrenbach enjoyed the connection between her love for technology and her subject, feeling that "it all comes together."

Finally, the vibrant and supportive UX community kept Bill Albert and Kevin Liang engaged in the field. His first conference energized Bill, reflecting, "There was just like a buzz, all this cool and interesting stuff." At the same time, Kevin appreciated the community's supportive nature, saying, "If it weren't for the community, I wouldn't have landed and gotten where I am."

1.6 Summary

As we have seen, UX is a broad field with people from diverse academic and professional backgrounds. Most of our UX Titans navigated through related fields like psychology, design, engineering, or information technology. Some came from unrelated backgrounds, like being in the army or working as a photographer.

While their backgrounds and previous jobs vary, they all share a commitment to improving people's lives through product and service design.

Another vital topic for several Titans is the dynamic and varied nature of UX.

While digging deeper, we realized that all our Titans stumbled into UX by chance, dissatisfaction with their former tasks, or curiosity. They often began with a broader purpose, such as a passion for ingenious product design or a desire to make a significant impact. They then found their way to UX to fulfill that goal.

There was no fastest and best way to enter UX for our Titans, and they had no specific (academic) background to be more likely to become a Titan. We also learned that our Titans stayed in the field because of the constant variety, challenges, and discovery. Many also like that they design for real impact and that their work makes a difference in people's lives.

1.7 Our thoughts

Looking at our Titan's journeys, one thing stands out: there was no straight line into UX back then – and we think that's still true today. Now, there are more ways to get into the field than ever. You've got dedicated "Human Factors" master's programs, high-quality online video academies, and countless other resources our Titans didn't have when they started. So, the paths into UX have multiplied, not simplified. They've become more diverse, not more straightforward. We see this as a good thing – it means more doors are open for anyone with a passion to jump in.

But with all these options, the big questions linger: How do you start in UX and grow into a true professional? How do you keep evolving once you're in?

If you're not in UX yet but wondering if it's your calling, we've got you covered. Based on the insights of this book, we've put together some guidance in Chapter 17 to help you figure that out – feel free to jump there now or keep reading through the book. Either way works!

For those of you already in UX or aspiring to be a UX Titan, here's what this means: you don't need to follow one "perfect" path. Start with what drives you – maybe a love for excellent product design, a fascination with technology, or a desire to improve people's lives through unforgettable experiences. Let UX be the way you bring that passion to life. Your journey can be as unique as you are, shaped by your interests and ambitions.

Don't stress about having a "traditional" route into UX. Focus on building the skills, curiosity, and adaptability to help you thrive. Your unique background can be your greatest strength. After all, UX is where it is today because of the diverse perspectives and contributions that have shaped it.

Of course, the road won't always be smooth – there'll be some twists and turns along the way. But that's part of the adventure. Let's jump into the next chapter to explore the Titans' roles and what helped them navigate those bumps a little easier.

2

Navigating daily UX: What do our Titans do, and what could have made their journey smoother?

Chapter two

Navigating daily UX: What do our Titans do, and what could have made their journey smoother?

2.1 What to expect from this chapter

In this chapter, we'll dive into the lessons our UX Titans have learned – insights they wish they had known at the start of their careers. Through their experiences, you'll uncover the challenges and key takeaways that have shaped their journeys in the UX field. The chapter offers insights into the essentials of a smooth UX journey, including navigating the tension between perfectionism and iterative development, balancing the human and technological aspects of UX, and the significance of careful career path planning. By the end of this chapter, you will see how learning and growing in UX is as rewarding as reaching the destination itself.

But before we examine the wisdom our UX Titans shared to make their daily UX tasks smoother, we want to learn more about their daily work.

2.2 The role of UX in our Titan's daily professional life

We asked our UX Titans how UX impacts their daily work and whether it has remained central to their professional roles. Here is what they shared:

Five Titans actively promote UX and empower teams by creating awareness and enabling their efforts. Guido Meier-Arendt and Oliver Kulpi, for example, focus on strategic UX, working to raise awareness and embed user-centered design within organizations. Tobias Oberpaul[15] supports his UX team by minimizing disruptions, while Katja Busch helps organizations become more people-centered. Kevin Liang experiences UX in all aspects of life, including everyday situations, and he reflects this in his mentoring and through his channels as an influencer.

[15] Tobias Oberpaul is a UX leader with a proven track record of driving digital transformation at Deutsche Bahn (DB) and as co-founder of the design studio SOVYY. Currently leading DB UX, he shapes the UX strategy across the company, fostering collaboration, transparency, and consistency through initiatives like the UX Design System. His extensive experience in creating user-centered digital solutions and leading cross-functional teams positions him as a key influencer and a Titan in the UX field.

Five Titans are deeply involved in UX work at the product or system level. Carmen Fehrenbach works in a 16-person UX team that enhances customer's user experiences. That is similar to Gert-Dieter Tuzar's work. Matthias Schulz[16] also enhances user experiences. However, he focuses not on customers' products but on internal IT solutions that co-workers use. The focus might differ, but their roles require daily UX design and research involvement, ensuring a great UX in their organizations.

[16] Matthias Schulz is a Senior UX Strategist and Researcher with extensive experience at Porsche AG and Mercedes-Benz, specializing in UX strategy, research, and sustainable maturity development within organizations. He leads UX initiatives, integrates user-centered design into agile frameworks, and mentors teams through training and awareness programs. With a strong background in psychology, design, and IT, Matthias also lectures at the Hochschule für Technik Stuttgart, sharing his expertise in usability and consumer research. His work and leadership in UX make him a standout figure in the field, driving innovation and measurable outcomes in user experience design.

Four Titans play crucial roles in leadership and management. Thomas Voehringer-Kuhnt[17] and Bill Albert manage UX teams, focusing on improving processes and methodologies. Ulf Schubert has transitioned from operational UX to organizational management, ensuring UX remains dynamic and relevant.

[17] Dr. Thomas Vöhringer-Kuhnt is a UX leader and mentor with extensive experience in the automotive industry, having held key roles at Mazda Motor Europe, Geely/Lotus Tech Innovation Centre, and Continental. He specializes in Human-Machine Interface (HMI) and UX design, mentoring emerging professionals at CareerFoundry and hosting the "Lead UX - The User Experience Leadership Circle" podcast. Driven by a passion for improving user experiences, he combines his deep expertise in product development and UX leadership to shape the future of user-centered design.

All other Titans have expanded beyond traditional UX roles. Oliver Kulpi has moved into strategy, while Marc Hassenzahl[18] and Sarah Diefenbach[19] have moved into academia. Lutz Krauß, Nis Boy Naeve, and Dominique Winter have taken on broader roles, incorporating UX principles into product experience and organizational development.

[18] Marc Hassenzahl is a leading expert in UX and Professor for "Ubiquitous Design" at the University of Siegen. With a Ph.D. in Psychology, he has held influential roles at institutions like the University of Koblenz-Landau, Folkwang University of Arts, and Siemens, shaping the field of experience and interaction design. His pioneering research focuses on creating pleasurable and meaningful interactive technologies, blending psychological insights with design. Hassenzahl's contributions have made him a prominent figure in UX, influencing both academic theory and practical design approaches.

In summary, the backgrounds of our Titans and how they experience, share, and evangelist UX in their daily working life differ. While some of them still participate in designing great UX on a product level, many of our Titans have switched roles to a meta-UX level, where they share their knowledge and enable others. This also shows our Titans' curiosity, the desire for constant learning and improvement, and the openness of the field, which enables constant change. And now, it is time to jump into the central part of this chapter: their lessons learned.

2.3 These are things our Titans wish they had known earlier in their careers.

2.3.1 Learning 1: The importance of convincing direct stakeholders

One of the most significant lessons that many of our UX Titans learned is the importance of advocating for UX from the beginning and dealing with direct stakeholders. Convincing customers, partners, and internal stakeholders of the value of UX is essential but often challenging. Four out of nineteen Titans highlighted that they wish they had known how crucial and difficult this would be earlier in their careers.

Sarah Diefenbach recalls the early challenges of establishing the importance of UX, especially in environments where companies were primarily focused on usability. Reflecting on her journey, she shared, "It was difficult initially, especially in projects with companies more concerned with usability... I remember exhausting conversations where you had to fight hard to include [UX] as a relevant question." Despite these challenges, her dedication to advancing UX and psychological ergonomics has been consistent throughout her career.

Carmen Fehrenbach adds that storytelling is often critical. "I would have liked to have known beforehand how much storytelling is involved [...] how often you have to sell your ideas," she shared. Carmen learned throughout her journey that effectively conveying design concepts through storytelling is essential for gaining stakeholder support and driving user-centered innovations. Gabriela Gomes agrees: "Good storytelling is the secret sauce to gain support from stakeholders and keep them engaged."

Similarly, Kerstin Dyck emphasizes that the real challenge lies in convincing others of the necessity of a user-centered process. She would have loved to know sooner "[...] how difficult it will be for years to come to convince many people that you need to ask users in a user-centered process. (laughs)". Despite her years in the field, she still finds it challenging to navigate the resistance from stakeholders who may need to thoroughly understand or prioritize user-centered UX methodologies.

Finally, Katja Busch reflects on the importance of understanding power dynamics when advocating for UX. "It took me a long time to understand how power works [...] Many UXers fight for a good cause, but some stakeholders want to retain their privileges [...] I learned to analyze and question these contexts with the empathy that comes with UX. If I had known this ten years earlier, I would have needed much less energy to find solutions," she concluded.

2.3.2 Learning 2: The importance of convincing indirect stakeholders and other people within the company

Besides convincing direct stakeholders, there is also a challenge in convincing **indirect** stakeholders of UX. This challenge can lead to much internal political work to incorporate UX practices within the company's development process.

This struggle is further echoed by Lutz Krauß, who emphasizes the challenges posed by decision-makers unfamiliar with design. "Many people who have no idea about design [...] have a say. And unfortunately, they are often higher in the hierarchy [...] That's the worst," he noted. Lutz underscores the need for design expertise at all levels of decision-making to drive UX innovation effectively.

Guido Meier-Arendt wishes he had better understood how to approach the various parties involved in the development process in general. "I would have liked to know more about the different mindsets of engineers, mechanics, and software developers [...] and how to approach them when advocating for UX," he remarked.

Thomas Voehringer-Kuhnt reflects on his early naivety in thinking that UX was straightforward. With years of experience, he now understands the political nature of UX within organizations.

"I thought it must be clear to everyone that we want to design technology that solves user problems. But 'that's not true [...] It's always about who makes decisions and how they are made, and they are not always rational," he noted.

As Uwe Betzin stresses, communication is vital in advocating for UX. "Communication is an essential skill of UX-ers [...] At some point, I realized I talk about my designs much more than I do design work," he explained, highlighting the unexpected importance of communication with all kinds of indirect (and direct) stakeholders in his role as a UX professional.

2.3.3 Learning 3: Change and user-centricity do not happen overnight.

Many UX Titans wish they had known that change within companies, especially toward a user-centric approach, only occurs gradually. Ulf Schubert learned this firsthand, recalling how he once believed he could drive change quickly: "You go in there, do things, and think: Yes, they've understood. And then you look back five years later and realize they haven't." He discovered that patience is crucial, as sometimes the right moment to advocate for UX only comes when something goes wrong. Ulf Schubert emphasizes that building a user-centered culture often requires long-term persistence and adapting strategies based on evolving organizational needs and stakeholder perspectives.

Matthias Schulz echoed this, explaining that in-house UX departments often face internal processes that slow down change: "I had to learn a lot of acceptance, tolerance, and how it just works." He elaborated that managing UX within large organizations involves driving UX strategy and research and overcoming resistance from stakeholders who may resist change to maintain their privileges. This makes pushing for a user-centric approach a challenging and time-consuming but essential task.

Guido Meier-Arendt pointed out that the speed of change often depends on a 'company's history and structure, requiring UX professionals to "be extremely patient." Carmen Fehrenbach wished she had known earlier how much effort it takes to educate others about UX, although she noted some progress over the years.

Finally, Bill Albert advised those new to the field to "play the long game." He emphasized that achieving impactful user experiences requires patience and a strategic approach, noting that "the best solutions come from working within the system and building strong relationships." Bill Albert stressed that delivering perfect user experiences involves navigating complex organizational dynamics and collaborating effectively over time.

2.3.4 Learning 4: Iterations over perfectionism

For two Titans, overcoming the struggle between perfectionism and iterative development was a pivotal lesson. Tobias Oberpaul admitted, "In my early career, perfectionism often hindered me." He learned that embracing iterative processes involving continuous feedback and refinement is far more effective for creating impactful digital solutions. His experience, reaching from refining design systems to managing agile teams, underscored the value of incrementally evolving designs rather than striving for unattainable perfection from the start.

Kevin Liang echoed this sentiment, advising his younger self "not to burden myself with the weight of having things perfect." Instead, he suggests embracing a tactical approach, treating everything as a draft, and continuously seeking feedback. Throughout his career, Kevin Liang has learned that iterative refinement and collaboration are essential, and he constantly underscores the value of empiricism and humility.

2.3.5 Learning 5: The journey is the reward.

Two Titans, Dominique Winter and Marc Hassenzahl, believe their learning journeys were valuable without shortcuts. Dominique mused, "I wouldn't have been able to do anything with today's knowledge five years ago without the journey there," emphasizing the importance of the process. Marc agreed, stating that his career's sequence of events and lessons "happened bit by bit, and that feels good."

2.3.6 Learning 6: Understanding human behavior and technology is crucial in UX

Gabriela Gomes realized later in her career that a deeper understanding of human behavior and technology (and how they interact) is crucial in UX. She reflected, "When I started in the late 2000s, early 2010s, the focus was on learning the latest graphic tools or prototyping and mastering interfaces, and I also came from the artistic side. So, there was a transition for me. [...] I could have benefited from spending a little more time on the fundamentals of human behavior or psychology, a little more science and engineering, because UX is obviously about designing the interaction between a human and a service or a product."

Gabriela also emphasized that integrating insights about human behavior and behavioral psychology can significantly enhance design outcomes. Her realization highlights the importance of a solid foundation in these areas, which can bridge gaps between user needs and technological solutions, ultimately leading to more impactful and user-friendly products.

2.3.7 Learning 7: Clarity on career paths and roles

Gert-Dieter Tuzar wished he had known about the various career paths available within UX, particularly those outside the traditional management track. He explained, "I didn't realize until very late that I have my strengths more in expertise and not so much in administrative skills." Gert-Dieter recognized that his true passion and strength lay in deepening his expertise rather than navigating administrative roles. This realization came after years of experience in both design and strategic roles.

2.4 Summary

This chapter has taken us into our UX Titans' daily lives and hard-earned wisdom, revealing the diverse ways they engage with UX and the lessons they wish they had grasped earlier in their careers. From hands-on design and research to strategic advocacy and leadership, the Titans' roles illustrate the breadth of the UX field and its evolving nature. Their experiences highlight a common thread: navigating the complexities of UX requires more than technical skill – it demands patience, adaptability, and a deep understanding of people and systems.

In addition to that, our UX Titans wish they had understood or known some things sooner in their career to make their profession a little more streamlined. Here are those pieces of wisdom that our Titans wish they had earlier on:

- **Communication:** An essential part of UX is to convince direct and indirect stakeholders like customers, partners, and decision-makers of the value of UX as soon as possible. Therefore, it is vital to understand their mindsets and goals.
- **Storytelling:** Communication comes on a one-on-one basis but also needs to be driven by ongoing storytelling that is integrated into all parts of the daily work. This includes finding powerful storylines that evangelists UX topics and design.
- **Play the long game:** Establishing change and user-centricity within a company takes time. All Titans involved in promoting UX within their companies would have loved to know earlier how long it would take.
- **It's all a draft:** Learning to embrace iterative design can be challenging when coming from disciplines where perfectionism is highly valued. However, perfectionism can be counterproductive regarding UX with its iterative

approach. Letting go of one's work and embracing "good enough for the moment" is a significant learning process that helps early on.

- **Humans and technology:** UX is a very multidisciplinary field. Independent of the personal background, having a profound knowledge of basic psychological and technological concepts helps to succeed in this field, where both are needed.

A lot of paths ahead: Being aware of UX's different career paths early on can help lighten the personal burden. As we've also seen in Chapter 1, there is no single path to success and greatness. Knowing that you are free to choose the best path can help you grow in the right direction.

Nonetheless, there are two Titans that, even if they could, would not want to change their journey. For them, a good journey needs no shortcuts but is crafted out of all experiences along the way!

2.5 Our thoughts

From our point of view, we could not agree more with our Titans. All points mentioned resonate with our experience. But we also want to highlight one crucial point our Titans pointed out: communication.

Communication is crucial for succeeding in UX (and most other areas). Sadly, communication is often viewed as just basic listening or talking. Therefore, it is often not taught in (higher) school forms. The result: projects fail. Not because of

UX / engineering / or whatever expert skill. They fail because of communication. And this is not a tiny percentage of complicated projects. According to a study from PMI[20], 56% of all projects fail due to poor communication.

So, if effective communication in UX isn't just about listening and speaking – what is it about? It's about bridging the gap between designers, engineers, stakeholders, and users. This bridge requires empathy, clear articulation of ideas, and the ability to adapt messages for different audiences. Learning to communicate with different disciplines and stakeholders helps master UX projects successfully. UX, in particular, involves many people on board, who usually need to be convinced, excited, or trained. Suppose you have no formal training or perceive problems in this area. In that case, it might be worth considering taking specialized communication courses focusing on cross-functional collaboration, active listening, and persuasion techniques. Role-playing exercises with different stakeholder types – even if often intensely disliked - can be a great way to sharpen these skills.

Besides communication, we want to add another detail from our perspective. We also made the experience that convincing stakeholders to do user testing and user research can be challenging. This is even more true if stakeholders never experience user testing but "just" look at the results. Our best way of convincing stakeholders is to get them to observe one user

[20] Monkhouse, P. (2015). My project is failing, it is not my fault. Paper presented at PMI® Global Congress 2015 – EMEA, London, England. Newtown Square, PA: Project Management Institute.

testing session. We typically get this learning curve (on a design/ product never tested with users before):

- Stakeholder on the first test person: "This one must be foolish. No one would behave like that."
- Stakeholder on the second test person: "Again, such a stupid user."
- Stakeholder on the third: "Where do you get such people? Again, a stupid one..."
- Stakeholder on the fourth one: *silence*
- Stakeholder on the fifth one: "F***, we have a problem."
- ...
- Stakeholder after the session: "I don't know how we could have ever worked without user testing. We answered so many questions we had. We will test again soon. „

From our experience, helping people gain first-hand experience of the power of UX is one of the best "communication tricks" we have so far discovered. You can probably leverage this as well or even have some other tricks to improve the UX of the UX.

3

Dream collaborations in UX: Who and why?

Chapter three

Dream collaborations in UX: Who and why?

3.1 What to expect from this chapter

Imagine this: If you could choose anyone in the world to collaborate with on a UX project, who would it be and why? Our UX Titans faced this exact question, and their answers reveal much more than just a list of famous names. They expose the qualities, values, and mindsets necessary for creating world-class UX partnerships – and, in doing so, provide valuable lessons for anyone looking to grow in the field.

In this chapter, you'll gain insights into the attributes that these leading experts prioritize when choosing their collaborators. You'll discover that the secret of evolving in UX isn't about chasing status or recognition – it's about seeking partnerships that challenge you, push your boundaries, and spark creativity. By exploring their dream collaborations, we'll uncover what drives impactful teamwork in UX and how these principles can shape your approach to the field.

3.2 Collaborations to learn from

Our Titans' dream collaborations reflect their curiosity and passion for growth, whether through specific individuals or inspiring qualities in a team. Here's who – or what – they'd choose and why:

Uwe Betzin views the partnership as a way to assess his skills and discover his blind spots: "To learn and also to get a self-assessment: Where do I stand? And where are we going with UX? I recognize what I haven't thought about yet and still have my blind spots."

With his background at SAP, Nis Boy Naeve focuses on expanding his horizons: "What I would enjoy is broadening my horizons. I've spent much time in the software environment making tangible products."

Bill Albert seeks partners who bring fresh perspectives and push boundaries: "I want to work with people from different perspectives. People who ask interesting questions, are creative problem solvers, and work on interesting products or spaces."

Carmen Fehrenbach looks for creative sparks: "I always like it when I feel there's something creative in it, some idea that's not run-of-the-mill."

Gert-Dieter Tuzar prioritizes teams motivated to create change and tackle new challenges: "I prefer to work with teams that are motivated to change something, to tackle something new. I enjoy exchanging ideas with people like Michaela [Kauer-Franz] and Ralph Bruder."

As a UX consultant, Katja Busch would choose the late Clayton Christensen, admiring his intellect and experience: "If I have to choose any person, it would be Clayton Christensen, author of the innovator's dilemma and populariser of the jobs-to-be-done method. His experience and intelligence in analyzing companies and markets would help us rethink UX tools and strategies."

With many years of experience as an educator, influencer, and UX manager, Kevin Liang recalls learning from Tom Tullis, whose quirky teaching style left a lasting impression: "Tom Tullis... I wish everybody could learn from him. He always made jokes at the beginning of a class, and his approach was brilliant."

Ulf Schubert values learning from people who have made significant contributions in the field: "I build networks and try to bring people together, finding those who have made things happen and learning from their approach, especially in terms of speed."

Marc Hassenzahl finds working with young minds enriching: "I enjoy working with young people. They bring such different perspectives, and I always find that enriching."

Thomas Vöhringer-Kuhnt said: "I'd love to work with the big gurus, you know? Don Norman, Jared Spool, and Jakob Nielsen – really collaborate with them one-on-one. That would be fascinating. These are people who have shaped not just the field but also the way we approach it, both conceptually and practically. For instance, imagine sitting down with Don Norman and hearing firsthand about his time at Apple – how he introduced ideas that we now call 'User Experience.' How did he manage to establish those concepts back then? That's something I'd really like to discuss with him."

Lutz Krauß also admires icons like Don Norman and Jakob Nielsen. He states: "I would have said Don Norman or Jakob Nielsen. I want to learn from them how they approach UX."

The common theme across all these responses is the importance of learning from others. Whether through gaining new perspectives, challenging the status quo, meeting with the people who have shaped the field, or being inspired by creativity, these Titans seek partnerships that fuel their personal and professional growth.

To conclude this chapter, let us look at the complete list of names our UX Titans shared as partners they would love to do UX with.

3.3 Without further ado, here are the names of all the people our UX Titans would love to collaborate and do UX with

- Jakob Nielsen (mentioned 3-times)
- Marc Hassenzahl (mentioned 3-times)
- Don Norman (mentioned 2-times)
- Jared Spool (mentioned 2-times)
- Michaela Kauer-Franz (mentioned 2-times, but this might be a bit biased ;))
- Sarah Diefenbach (mentioned 2-times)
- Ulf Schubert (mentioned 2-times)
- Bill Gaver
- Clayton Christensen (RIP)

- Dana Chisnell
- Jack Caroll
- James Lewis
- Jeff Sauro
- Markus Mündel
- Matthias Zabka
- Peter Merholz
- Ralph Bruder
- Shigeru Miyamoto
- Stefanie Weber
- Thomas Immich
- Tom Tullis (RIP)

3.4 Summary

This chapter uncovers the dream collaborations of our UX Titans, revealing the values behind their choices. When asked who – or what – they'd partner with, they shun fame or profit for growth, creativity, and impact, whether through specific individuals or team qualities.

Learning drives many selections. Uwe Betzin sees collaboration as a self-assessment tool, uncovering blind spots, while Nis Boy Naeve wants to expand beyond his SAP software roots. Bill Albert craves fresh perspectives from creative problem-solvers, and Thomas Vöhringer-Kuhnt and Lutz Krauß both name Don Norman and Jakob Nielsen, eager to learn from their field-shaping approaches – Norman's Apple innovations or Nielsen's usability breakthroughs.

Creativity and change also stand out. Carmen Fehrenbach seeks "creative sparks" in unconventional ideas, and Gert-Dieter Tuzar favors teams motivated to disrupt, citing Michaela Kauer-

Franz and Ralph Bruder. Katja Busch picks Clayton Christensen for his market-altering intellect, imagining new UX strategies, while Kevin Liang recalls Tom Tullis's brilliant, humorous teaching.

Connections span generations, too. Marc Hassenzahl values young minds' "enriching" views, and Ulf Schubert seeks those who've made an impact with speed. The 3.3 list – led by Nielsen and Hassenzahl (three mentions each), Norman (two), and others like Christensen and Shigeru Miyamoto – reflects this range. Ultimately, these Titans choose partners who fuel curiosity and innovation, proving UX thrives on learning and bold collaboration.

3.5 Our thoughts

The Titans' dream collaborations show how much they crave learning, and we agree with that. UX is a lot about learning. But we would also like to show another side of learning our Titans did not mention directly. Let us share a story from Ben's perspective:

At university, I was an engineer churning out user interfaces – logical, efficient, and flawless, in my opinion. They worked, technically – but users hated them. For them, my user interfaces were not logical at all. They were hard to use and cumbersome. That's when a teammate with a background in psychology stepped in. This teammate (who happened to be Michaela, by the way) challenged my user interfaces in a way I had never experienced before. Sometimes, her solutions were the opposite of mine. But most importantly, hers worked with users.

But she didn't just tweak my designs; she challenged my whole lens, forcing me to question what I thought "good" meant. I loved and hated it at the same time. With Michaela's help, we made user interfaces that users loved. And I learned a lot about the user's perspective – and myself.

That's the thing: having someone challenge your view, like Michaela did for me, can shake you up in a good way. It's not always comfortable; it might even hurt, depending on how much you like being right, but it moves you forward. Fast. There's a saying I love: "If you're the smartest person in the room, you're in the wrong room." Michaela got me out of mine, and I think the Titans are after someone who does that for them, too, even if it hurts sometimes.

One additional remark: With the rise of AI tools, new ways exist to challenge your ideas. An AI can be a relentless and swift sparring partner. But don't forget to test your ideas with users nevertheless.

So, if challenging our views – whether by people or tools like AI – drives us forward, how does that shape the stuff we create? In the next chapter, we'll shift gears to explore what our Titans consider UX masterpieces – those standout products and services – and unpack the traits that make them shine. Get ready to see how their lessons play out in the real world.

4

UX masterpieces – what are the characteristics of services or products with an outstanding UX?

Chapter four

UX masterpieces – what are the characteristics of services or products with an outstanding UX?

4.1 What to expect from this chapter

So far, we've explored our Titans' backgrounds, the lessons they wish they'd learned earlier, and their dream collaborations. Now, we turn to what they see as great UX. In this chapter, we asked our UX Titans about products and services they love – ones they consider outstanding – and why they stand out.

They gave us a goldmine of stories, from everyday apps to clever gadgets and services, each packed with insights into what makes UX click. We've taken the whole list and teased out key characteristics that define UX masterpieces. By the end, you'll walk away with practical ideas to shape designs that hit home with users.

4.2 What makes UX stand out?

Here are the answers of our Titans and the characteristics we've drawn from them:

4.2.1 The invisible power of simplification

For many of our Titans, the hallmark of great UX is its ability to strip away complexity and make users feel effortlessly in control. It's not just about making tasks faster; it's about designing intuitive and almost invisible interactions – like magic at the user's fingertips.

Simplification means turning tangled tasks into effortless wins and allowing users to focus on what matters. As Gabriela Gomes points out, it's about transforming time-consuming processes into seamless interactions. She highlights how today's apps have mastered this: "Now it's two taps on my phone to send money or one tap to play music. Google Photos[21] stores and curates my photos automatically." The beauty of these solutions lies in their ability to integrate into daily life without feeling intrusive or demanding.

For Nis Boy Naeve, personalization without hassle is an essential element. Reflecting on his experience with Bang & Olufsen speakers[22], he recalls being amazed by how the system instantly adjusted to the surroundings: "With one click, the

[21] Google Photos is a tool that allows users to store, share, view, and edit photos and videos while providing AI-powered tools for organization and enhancements.

[22] Bang & Olufsen speakers are high-end audio products known for their exceptional sound quality, innovative design, and premium craftsmanship.

system personalized the sound experience for me. Within half a minute, it was perfectly tailored to the room." This effortless setup transformed what could have been a tedious calibration into a fast, simple, and delightful experience.

Thomas Vöhringer-Kuhnt sees the magic of simplification in creative contexts. He shares his experience with GarageBand[23], where the tool doesn't demand expert knowledge but instead empowers creativity: "I plug in my microphone, press a few buttons, and have great sound. It's incredibly easy for music enthusiasts like me." This is one example where a product becomes almost invisible – it supports without overshadowing the creative process, turning complex audio engineering into a simple, joyful activity.

Matthias Schulz echoes this sentiment when describing the VVS app[24] that simplifies public transportation in parts of Germany: "It's easy enough for my whole family to use, allowing us to order tickets or track transport instantly." For this product, the key lies in removing unnecessary steps and focusing on quick, reliable outcomes that any user can achieve regardless of their tech skills.

Kevin Liang reflects on a product that simplifies something traditionally intimidating – car tuning: "It gives clear, intuitive directions, even though I'm no mechanic. It's like magic." By translating technical jargon into clear guidance, this tool transforms a specialized task into something approachable and unintimidating.

[23] GarageBand is a digital audio workstation developed by Apple that allows users to create, record, edit, and produce music or podcasts.

[24] The VVS app, provided by the Verkehrs- und Tarifverbund Stuttgart, Germany (VVS), is a mobile application designed for public transportation users in the Stuttgart region. It allows users to plan routes, view real-time schedules, and purchase tickets.

On the other hand, Katja Busch appreciates Apple products' efficiency and reliability, especially when it matters most: "My Mac[25] always works smoothly without needing IT support, saving time during critical moments." This reliability under pressure, makes the technology feel almost invisible – allowing users to focus on their tasks rather than the tool itself.

Uwe Betzin highlights how iterative improvements have transformed Microsoft Outlook[26] from a clunky tool to an efficient powerhouse: "They listen to feedback and fix problems quickly, making the user experience much better." This continuous refinement means users don't have to fight against outdated or cumbersome designs (at least for long), preserving their time and energy for meaningful work.

Finally, Bill Albert offers another example of seamless UX: "I bought some Apple AirTags[27], and I was amazed by how effortless the setup was. In seconds, it was ready to go, and now I just toss one in my luggage and can track it without any stress. What I love most is that it's small, simple, and reduces anxiety without drawing attention to itself. That's great UX – it works so well that you barely notice it. Good design should blend in like that."

---

[25] A Mac is Apple's line of computers known for their sleek design, macOS operating system, and suitability for creative and productivity tasks.

[26] Microsoft Outlook is an email client and personal information manager developed by Microsoft. It offers tools for sending and receiving emails, managing calendars, contacts, tasks, and notes.

[27] Apple AirTags are small, coin-sized tracking devices designed to help users locate personal items such as keys, bags, or wallets.

4.2.2 Emotional experience over pure functionality

In some products, the user experience goes beyond mere functionality, focusing instead on how the product feels and interacts with the user on an emotional level. Many Titans highlight this approach, choosing products that prioritize experience over function.

Lutz Krauß shares an example he often showcases to illustrate an exceptional user experience: "I have a button that I always show in my talks. It used to be sold by Staples. It's a big silver button with a red top, and when you press it, it says 'That was easy!' in a cheerful tone. It's a clever UX – instant feedback, tactile satisfaction, and accessibility. The button is large enough for anyone, including older people, to use easily, and the whole experience leaves you with a sense of accomplishment. It really feels like everything was just... easy."

Marc Hassenzahl brings forward two products that subtly but effectively meet an essential human need: "My favorite example is the Philips Wake-Up Light[28]. It's just an alarm clock with a lamp. There's nothing fancy about the design or interaction. In my version, you can't even set the alarm time – it just starts glowing 30 minutes before your wake-up time. But the experience it creates is so different from a regular alarm clock. It feels natural, almost like waking up with the sunrise. The second example is a bit unusual – a line of couple's products that included sex toys. They only launched in Italy, but it's interesting because they addressed

[28] A Philips Wake-up Light is a lamp designed to simulate a natural sunrise to help users wake up more gradually and feel more refreshed. It gradually increases in brightness over a set period, mimicking the sunrise, and may also include soothing sounds or nature noises.

an essential human experience that often gets overlooked in product design."

Carmen Fehrenbach reflects on a household product feature that adds a new dimension to an everyday task: "I recently bought a Dyson vacuum[29] cleaner. To be honest, I was a bit underwhelmed, given the price. However, one thing that really stood out was the green laser light feature. When you vacuum in the dark, it highlights the dust on the floor, and there's something oddly satisfying about seeing the dust disappear as you go over it. Sure, I could do the same thing with a flashlight, but it's still a fun experience. That said, the vacuum itself isn't that powerful compared to my old one, and the batteries run out quickly, so I sometimes wonder if I got caught up in the novelty of the laser rather than focusing on the vacuum's performance. Still, it adds a unique touch to an otherwise mundane chore."

4.2.3 Rethinking common problems

For four of our nineteen Titans, innovation often starts by looking at everyday problems from a new perspective. By rethinking solutions, they've crafted products with outstanding user experiences. This approach shows that even if a product's components aren't entirely new, reimagining how they come together can evoke positive emotions, redefine user expectations, and create a good UX. Identifying user needs that others may have

[29] A Dyson vacuum is a high-performance cleaning device known for its advanced technology and powerful suction. These vacuums often feature bagless designs with cyclonic separation to capture fine dust and debris.

overlooked or dismissed can lead to game-changing solutions that feel fresh and revolutionary.

Ulf Schubert shares a Bosch Power Tools success story: "The IXO mini cordless screwdriver[30] – now a huge seller – started as an idea no one thought necessary. A small team used design thinking to identify the need, but the company was skeptical and focused on powerful drills. Yet, understanding user needs turned it into a massive hit." Unlike traditional heavy-duty drills, the IXO's lightweight and compact design made it ideal for small everyday household tasks, appealing to a broader, more inexperienced audience.

Marc Hassenzahl gives another example with the already mentioned Philips Wake-Up Light: "For years, alarm clocks were rigid and mechanical, despite everyone hating them. The Wake-Up Light's simple idea of waking up gently in sync with natural rhythms solved a real problem." The rethinking process was how to remove the alarm from the alarm clock – replacing it with a natural, gradual light that mimics the sunrise.

Tobias Oberpaul highlights how rethinking a common approach led to a new standard in mobile navigation: "Placing navigation at the bottom of a web app blurred the line between native and web apps. It was a fresh approach that showed true consideration for user needs."

In another example, Guido Meier-Arendt recalls the iPhone's[31] impact: "In 2009, the iPhone created magical moments, blending

---

[30] The IXO Mini Cordless Screwdriver by Bosch is a compact, versatile tool known for its user-friendly design for inexperienced users and unexpected success in the power tool market.

[31] An iPhone is a smartphone developed by Apple, known for its sleek design, advanced features, and integration with the Apple ecosystem.

existing elements – like the App Store and touch interface – into a bold, emotional user experience. It showed that great UX isn't just about new tech but rethinking how we use what's already there."

4.2.4 Cross-device functionality

In today's interconnected world, users expect seamless transitions between devices. Whether starting a task on a desktop, continuing on a tablet, or finishing on a smartphone, they want the experience to feel consistent and intuitive. Cross-device functionality is no longer a luxury – it's necessary for modern products that aim to be truly user-centric. Here are some examples highlighted by our Titans:

Gabriela Gomes highlights Peloton[32] as a standout example: "Peloton's cross-device experience goes beyond just fitness equipment. What I love about the Peloton experience is that it's designed to support users at every stage of their lives, whether recovering from an injury, battling illness, or just needing a quick session on the go. Its thoughtful programming and user-friendly cross-device experience make it easy to find exactly what you need, no matter where you are."

Tobias Oberpaul praises Airbnb[33] for setting a benchmark in cross-device innovation: "They blur the lines between native apps and the web, offering consistent navigation and innovation across platforms." What makes Airbnb exceptional is its ability to

[32] A Peloton bike is a high-end stationary exercise bike that offers live and on-demand fitness classes through its built-in touchscreen. It provides it's services also via the website or app.

[33] Airbnb is a global online marketplace for lodging, vacation rentals, and travel experiences, known for its intuitive platform that seamlessly integrates across mobile and web.

adapt to user context, whether they're browsing from a phone while traveling or planning a trip on a computer. By maintaining consistent functionality and familiar UI patterns across devices, Airbnb ensures that users feel at home regardless of how they interact with the service.

Kerstin Dyck highlights another part of cross-device convenience: "When our children were so small that we still carried them most of the time, I did everything on my phone with one hand – shopping, banking, copying numbers from bills. It's these little things that make life easier." Her example showcases how a changed user context moderates the need for different solutions and how cross-device functionality adds in.

4.2.5 Ease of learning

A great user experience goes beyond just being functional or visually appealing – it also needs to be easy to learn. Products that enable users to get started quickly and feel confident early on have a distinct advantage. This is especially crucial when the task at hand is complex or unfamiliar. Among our nineteen Titans, two highlight ease of learning as a critical element of exceptional usability and user experience:

Dominique Winter draws inspiration from the gaming world to illustrate how mental models and immersion can significantly accelerate learning: "Sure, I could mention Nintendo[34] games or others, but in general, video games excel at enabling fast progress

[34] Nintendo is a global leader in video game design, known for creating intuitive, player-friendly experiences through iconic franchises like Mario, Zelda, and Pokémon.

through elements like immersion and easily graspable mental models. These models often align with real-world experiences, making learning intuitive."

Similarly, Sarah Diefenbach brings up a product that offers real-time feedback, helping users adjust and learn quickly: "It's a small example, but during my time working with Oral-B[35], I was impressed by their electric toothbrushes. One feature I appreciated was the indicator ring that would let you know – without much effort – if you were brushing too hard, too gently, or just right. The immediate feedback allows users to adapt their technique almost instinctively."

4.3 Another angle: Is there really such a thing as outstanding UX?

After discussing many examples of great UX, we would like to take a step back and consider a different perspective. While many of our Titans shared stories of products they admired, not everyone agreed that any product could exemplify outstanding UX. Some believe that even the most celebrated products fall short and that progress in the field has sometimes been slower than expected.

One of the most thought-provoking viewpoints comes from Gert-Dieter Tuzar, who expresses a rather sobering perspective on the state of UX today. He elaborates on his viewpoint:

"That's a tough question for me, and I have to respond with a resounding 'no,' which is quite regrettable. I'm not convinced

[35] Oral-B is a leading brand in oral hygiene, known for its innovative electric toothbrushes that provide real-time feedback to improve brushing technique.

by any single product out there. Take the automotive industry, for instance. In recent years, advancements in user experience within human-machine interfaces have taken a step backward rather than forward. It's baffling to consider – where have the last 30 or 40 years gone? Have we really learned anything at that time? I must admit, I'm left feeling disheartened by the lack of progress."

4.4 Summary

We asked our Titans to name products and services they consider outstanding regarding UX. Instead of just listing their answers, we analyzed their choices and identified recurring themes that point to the characteristics of exceptional UX:

- **The invisible power of simplification:** Many Titans emphasize how great UX often goes unnoticed because it works seamlessly. These products streamline complex tasks to the point of feeling almost invisible, reducing effort and time compared to other solutions.
- **Emotional experience over functionality:** Some products excel in creating emotional connections with users, prioritizing feelings over pure functionality. Examples include products like the Apple AirTag that provide immediate satisfaction and reduce anxiety or even household products like vacuum cleaners.
- **Rethinking common problems:** Several Titans discuss the power of innovative thinking to address everyday

challenges, leading to products that effectively meet overlooked user needs, for example, the IXO screwdriver.

- **Cross-device functionality:** Being able to switch between different devices seamlessly has a significant impact on the UX and enhances user experiences across different devices. Products like Peloton and Airbnb are highlighted for seamless integration and consistent platform usability.
- **Ease of learning:** A couple of Titans spotlight the importance of intuitive design and real-time feedback in learning. This is illustrated through examples from gaming and user-friendly health products.

Despite these insights, Gert-Dieter Tuzar presents a contrasting viewpoint, arguing that no single product universally exemplifies great UX. He expresses disappointment in the stagnation observed in areas like automotive user interfaces, indicating that while strides have been made, significant gaps still need to be in achieving an ideal user experience.

4.5 Our thoughts

Each Titan has provided unique perspectives on what constitutes outstanding UX, revealing a tapestry of characteristics that, when woven together, can significantly elevate the user experience. Our Titan's preferences directly reflect some of the well-known guidelines and processes in the field and show their power for the design of exceptional products. How can we apply these lessons to our daily work in the UX field? Here are some key takeaways for your daily work:

- **Always design with the user in mind:** At its core, exceptional UX begins with understanding the user's needs, challenges, and goals. Products that simplify complex tasks – like Google Photos, praised by Gabriela Gomes and or Bang & Olufsen speakers mentioned by Nis Boy Naeve – are rooted in deep empathy for the user. Start every project by engaging with real users through interviews, surveys, or usability tests. Use these insights to guide your decisions and ensure your design makes their lives easier and more enjoyable.
- **Simplicity is key:** Simplicity doesn't necessarily mean stripping away features – it means making interactions intuitive. Kevin Liang's example of a tablet for car tuning shows how clear, intuitive design can feel like magic. Continuously ask yourself, "How can I simplify this for the user?" When complexity is unavoidable, provide thoughtful guidance to ensure clarity.
- **Build for seamless experiences:** In our interconnected world, users often transition between devices. Products like Peloton and Airbnb excel by maintaining consistent usability across platforms. As you design, consider how your product fits into the broader ecosystem of user devices and contexts. A seamless experience fosters trust and loyalty.
- **Focus on emotional engagement:** Great UX is, at its core, about how a product makes users feel. Functionality is only one part of the story. Marc Hassenzahl's Philips Wake-Up Light and Bill Albert's Apple AirTags show the power

of creating emotional connections. To evoke positive emotions, incorporate moments of delight, surprise, or satisfaction into your designs. Thoughtful aesthetics, tactile feedback, and clever interactions can transform functional products into meaningful experiences.

- **Rethink the ordinary:** Some of the most innovative products come from looking at everyday challenges with fresh eyes. Ulf Schubert's story of the IXO cordless screwdriver demonstrates how reimagining user needs can lead to revolutionary solutions. Use tools like design thinking to challenge assumptions and explore alternative approaches to common problems.
- **Embrace iteration, not perfection:** Gert-Dieter Tuzar's perspective reminds us that no product can be perfect for everyone. Instead of striving for unattainable perfection, focus on continuous improvement. Gather user feedback, monitor emerging trends, and refine your designs over time. Growth is the hallmark of great UX. This is even more true when reminded that users' expectations are evolving, which constitutes great UX.

By embracing these principles, you can craft experiences that resonate with users and set your designs apart. The Titans remind us that UX excellence is not just about the end product but about the mindset, curiosity, and dedication fueling the journey. With that in mind, let us dive deeper and focus on how our UX Titans define UX.

5

Defining UX – how do our Titans think UX?

Chapter five

Defining UX – how do our Titans think UX?

5.1 What to expect from this chapter

In the last chapter, we explored what makes a product or service a UX masterpiece through the eyes of our UX Titans. Now, we take a step back to answer a fundamental question: What is UX?

Our UX Titans share their perspectives, revealing no one-size-fits-all answer. Instead, UX is an ever-evolving concept shaped by personal experiences, industry challenges, and philosophical reflections. This chapter uncovers how UX goes beyond mere usability, venturing into emotional connections, long-term impressions, and the intricate relationship between users and those who create their experiences.

We also address some of the most common misconceptions about UX, from confusing UI with UX to falsely equating UX with manipulation.

5.2 What is UX for our UX Titans?

We've sorted our Titan's answers into three buckets to answer that question. Let's start with the first one:

5.2.1 UX as a holistic journey: The emotional dimension

For many of our Titans, UX is about a user's entire journey with a product or service. It's a holistic experience that includes usability, emotional satisfaction, long-term engagement, and how users feel before, during, and after interacting with a product.

Bill Albert emphasizes: "UX is the user's overall experience with a product, especially in digital environments where there is some form of interface. It's the emotions, reactions, and perceptions users form that define the true nature of UX."

Uwe Betzin also draws on the emotional component when defining UX. Additionally, he adds motivation: "Software works," Uwe asserts, "when the user doesn't just do their job with it but wants to do it better."

Similarly, Tobias Oberpaul stresses the importance of an emotionally valuable connection: "In the end, it's the overall feeling. Did I achieve what I wanted and feel good about it? This emotional aspect is crucial to UX, transforming it from a functional exercise into an experience that users remember and value."

Carmen Fehrenbach's approach defines UX similarly: "It's not just about whether the system functions as expected but how it makes me feel throughout the process. Do I feel picked up? Do I feel relaxed and in control?" Carmen asks. According to her, a genuinely great UX does not leave users annoyed or frustrated, repeatedly pressing the same button, or unsure what to do next. Instead, it should create an environment where the user feels confident, capable, and even pleased with their interaction.

Gert-Dieter Tuzar echoes these sentiments, framing UX as a process designed to place the user at the heart of the development cycle. "It's about solving the problems users have with technology," Gert-Dieter explains. He focuses on creating an experience that works and feels natural and intuitive to the user, leading to greater technology acceptance. This requires balancing functionality with emotional satisfaction, an intricate dance between efficiency and ease of use, or what Gert-Dieter calls "functional beauty." For him, a successful UX "combines both aesthetic and emotional harmony," where the user tolerates the product and finds joy in using it.

Guido Meier-Ahrendt furthers this idea, arguing the design allows users to accomplish what they need without frustration in an environment that feels aesthetically pleasing and emotionally supportive. Guido discusses achieving a "perfect balance," where usability merges seamlessly with emotional and aesthetic qualities.

Thomas Voehringer-Kuhnt views UX with an even more holistic approach. He says UX is a "part of a more significant customer experience." Thomas believes every interaction users have with a brand, whether through products or services, contributes to their overall perception of the company. UX is not just about how easy or enjoyable a product is to use – "it's about how users experience the entire lifecycle of that brand interaction, from initial contact to long-term engagement."

5.2.2 UX as a "lasting impression."

In the last chapter, our Titans discussed UX as a holistic journey. This is also true for the citations we want to focus on in this section. In contrast to the last section, UX is seen here as experiences with one product that guide the general usage and experiences of the same and other product(s).

Kerstin Dyck suggests that "UX is more than just how a product functions. It's also about the lasting impression it leaves on users once they're done." She emphasizes the importance of the emotional aftermath: "Does the user feel drained after using the product? Or do they walk away feeling satisfied and confident, eager to use it again?" In her view, the "best UX leaves users with positive feelings, encouraging them to return to the same product or others without hesitation."

Katja Busch takes this concept even more profoundly by exploring the intersection of UX and neuropsychology. She explains that experiences, both good and bad, shape how users will interact with technology, a product, or a brand in the future. "There are good and bad UX," Busch explains, "and they create programs in the brain for future behavior. Bad experiences cost energy, so you, ideally, avoid them in the future. Routines and good experiences trigger rewards in the brain, and we want more of these endogenous drugs and like to do it again." To her, UX is not just about the moment of use but about how that experience stays in the brain of users, shaping their future interactions with technology and other systems.

5.2.3 UX is communication between the user and the product or even the designer and the product.

We already talked about Uwe Betzin's view on UX. However, there is another dimension in his philosophy: communication. He sees UX as a dynamic dialogue, but not between the user and the system, as one might expect. Instead, the real conversation is between the user and the team behind the software – the product designers, developers, and decision-makers. In this sense, the software reflects the choices and decisions made by these people, cast into code and set in stone. Users then face the challenge of interpreting these decisions, often leading to frustration when things do not align with their expectations. Uwe compares this communication breakdown to an old married couple, where each party talks past the other, struggling to connect.

"Our job is to facilitate that dialogue during the design and development process," Uwe continues. "True UX comes from understanding, communicating, and making decisions in the user's best interests." The ultimate goal is to create products that allow for a human-centered experience where the user feels engaged and empowered rather than confused or alienated. He emphasizes that a good UX professional must advocate for the user, becoming their voice within the product team and ensuring the design serves their needs.

5.3 Here are the things our UX Titans think are NOT UX.

The UX Titans' insights reveal how complex and multifaceted UX is. Therefore, we also asked our Titans about what is NOT UX and common misunderstandings. Here is what they answered:

5.3.1 UI is not UX

One of the most widespread misconceptions is the conflation of UX with UI (User Interface). As many of our UX Titans pointed out, the belief that UX is merely about making things "look good" or designing interfaces remains persistent.

Dominique Winter illustrates this classic mistake by recalling how companies often request both "UX/UI" as if they are interchangeable. He explains, "People don't understand that user experience is not just about making something pretty."

Sarah Diefenbach adds that UX is frequently reduced to "making the colors right." She laments that this focus on surface-level decisions misses the point: "UX should be about creating a positive experience." Marc Hassenzahl echoes this frustration, noting that "many approach UX design by following templates or adding standard features without considering the user's experience."

Lutz Krauß provides a memorable example from his work: "Endless debates over the most minor details in UI, like whether a transparency level should be 55% or 56%, often overshadow the bigger picture. " He points out that such details, while sometimes important, are not UX. Similarly, Nis Boy Naeve observes that some designers get too caught up in aesthetics – things that "look cool but are completely useless," which detracts from the overall user experience.

The metaphor from Thomas Vöhringer-Kuhnt is particularly vivid: "UI is like the tip of the iceberg – what users see. But UX is 80% of the submerged iceberg, all the elements behind the scenes that shape how users feel about their interaction." This iceberg metaphor highlights the distinction between UI's visible elements and the depth of UX, which includes research, interactions, and long-term emotional impact.

5.3.2 "UX" without users is not UX.

Several Titans expressed frustration with the growing trend of "shortcutting" UX, where teams claim to do UX simply by engaging in a few user-centered activities without involving actual users. Gabriela Gomes points out that methodologies like design thinking are often used as a quick fix: "Companies might sometimes use its methods and activities to feel like they're doing UX, but without user involvement, it's not the real thing. You can't just empathize with users by thinking about them; you need research to replace assumptions."

Kevin Liang stresses a similar view, highlighting the user-centricity and the iterative nature of UX: "It's not something you tick off once, and you're done. It's about continually asking questions and evolving the solution with users." Gert-Dieter Tuzar shares this sentiment, referring to the prevalence of "UX washing," a technique where companies superficially adopt UX practices without fully committing to the depth required for meaningful design.

Carmen Fehrenbach also cautions against taking shortcuts by relying on internal opinions: "UX isn't the opinion of the CEO or their spouse," she remarks humorously. "It's about the user's experience, which can't be shortcut by assumptions or internal feedback loops."

5.3.3 Manipulation is not UX.

Another misconception noted by Kerstin Dyck is that UX can sometimes be conflated with manipulation designed to get users to do things they do not want to do. She explains, "We're not trying to manipulate users into behaving a certain way. Instead, when we use behavioral psychology, it should guide users toward choices they want to make, like sustainable behaviors." Kerstin highlights that UX should help users, not deceive them, distinguishing the ethical lines UX must not cross.

Sarah Diefenbach also agrees with that. She mentioned that UX is often understood to optimize ad placement for revenue, but UX is "not just manipulating user behavior for profit."

5.3.4 Brand perception is not UX.

For some Titans, the public's perception of UX is too broad. Bill Albert draws a parallel between UX and medicine. While doctors treat individual patients, UX works at the level of personal interactions, whereas branding often deals with broader perceptions akin to public health. He explains, "Your perception of a brand is not UX. UX involves an interaction, something personal and specific."

This opinion contrasts with some holistic approaches of other Titans we discussed in 5.2.1.

5.4 Summary

So, what is UX according to our Titans? It is a dynamic blend of usability, emotional engagement, and intuitive communication. The key elements include:

- **UX as a holistic journey - The emotional dimension:** For many Titans, UX is more than just usability or functionality; it is a holistic journey encompassing how users feel before, during, and after interacting with a product. Bill Albert emphasizes that UX is shaped by user's emotions, reactions, and perceptions. Tobias Oberpaul and Uwe Betzin add that great UX motivates users to engage and strive for better outcomes. Thomas Voehringer-Kuhnt takes it further, seeing UX as an integral part of the customer experience, influencing long-term engagement and brand perception.
- **UX as a lasting impression:** Beyond the immediate interaction, some Titans view UX as a lasting impact that shapes future behavior. Kerstin Dyck highlights the importance of leaving users with positive feelings

that encourage them to return to the product. Katja Busch dives deeper, explaining how positive or negative experiences can form mental patterns that influence future interactions with the same or similar products. The key takeaway is that great UX creates lasting impressions that resonate beyond the moment of use.

- **UX as communication between users and products:** UX acts as a dynamic dialogue between users and the decisions made by designers, developers, and product teams. Uwe Betzin compares this relationship to an ongoing conversation, emphasizing the need for clear, intuitive communication in every interaction. The goal is to empower users, ensuring they feel understood and supported by the design.

In contrast, according to our Titans, UX is NOT:

- **UI is not UX:** While UI plays a role in UX, it is just the tip of the iceberg. UX encompasses the broader experience, including usability, emotional engagement, and long-term satisfaction. As Thomas Voehringer-Kuhnt reminds us, the actual depth of UX lies in the submerged portion of the iceberg – the research, interaction design, and emotional impact.
- **"UX" without users is not UX:** Genuine UX requires direct user involvement. Shortcuts like design thinking without research fail to capture the authentic needs of users. Gabriela Gomes explains that empathizing with users requires replacing assumptions with real insights.

Kevin Liang notes that iterative processes are essential for evolving solutions based on user feedback.

- **Manipulation is not UX:** Ethical UX design empowers users to make informed decisions rather than manipulating them into actions they do not want. Kerstin Dyck emphasizes that UX should guide users toward choices that align with their goals, ensuring trust and long-term satisfaction. Ethical boundaries are vital to maintaining the integrity and underlying values of UX design.
- **Brand perception is not UX:** While branding shapes public perception, UX focuses on individual interactions and their impact. Bill Albert draws a parallel to medicine: branding is like public health, while UX is akin to patient care – personal and specific. Distinguishing between these layers ensures clarity when designing user-centered experiences.

5.5 Our thoughts

Reflecting on the insights shared by our UX Titans, it becomes clear that UX is a deeply interconnected discipline, balancing usability, emotional engagement, and advocacy for the user. To expand on these perspectives, we find our UX Tree metaphor (Franz & Kauer-Franz 2024[36]) particularly useful. Let us explain:

Imagine a tree's roots – hidden beneath the surface but essential for survival. In the same way, ergonomics forms the unseen foundation of a successful user experience. A product must first be physically and cognitively comfortable, or everything else will fail.

[36] Franz, B., & Kauer-Franz, M. (2024). Usability and user experience design: The comprehensive guide to data-driven UX Design. Rheinwerk Publishing Inc.

For example, consider a pair of virtual reality goggles. No matter how immersive the experience, users will quickly become frustrated if the headset is heavy or awkward. Poor ergonomics can undermine even the best-designed systems.

Going up the roots, we have reached the trunk. In our metaphor, the trunk represents usability – the sturdy support system that connects the roots to the crown. Without usability, even the best-designed products fail to deliver value.

Usability ensures that users can achieve their goals effectively, efficiently, and satisfactorily. For example, a navigation app must quickly provide directions. The product's effectiveness falters if users cannot easily find their destination or interpret the interface. Like a tree's trunk, usability gives a product strength, durability, and consistency.

Let us look at the tree's crown. In our tree metaphor, the crown – its branches, leaves, and blossoms – symbolizes the emotional and experiential aspects of UX that captivate users. It is here that products transcend functionality, creating differentiation and inspiring loyalty. Just as the crown of a tree is its most visible and striking feature, the UX crown sets a product apart in users' eyes.

A flourishing crown addresses users' meaning, stimulation, and connection needs. For example, an app that allows users to organize cherished family photos effortlessly does not just perform a function – it evokes joy and strengthens bonds, creating an emotional attachment.

However, the crown's vibrancy depends on the strength of the roots (ergonomics) and trunk (usability). Even the most innovative or delightful features cannot sustain user satisfaction without a solid foundation. The UX crown is the culmination of a product's foundation and structure, and it serves as the differentiating factor that transforms a good product into an exceptional experience.

Here is the UX tree in all its beauty:

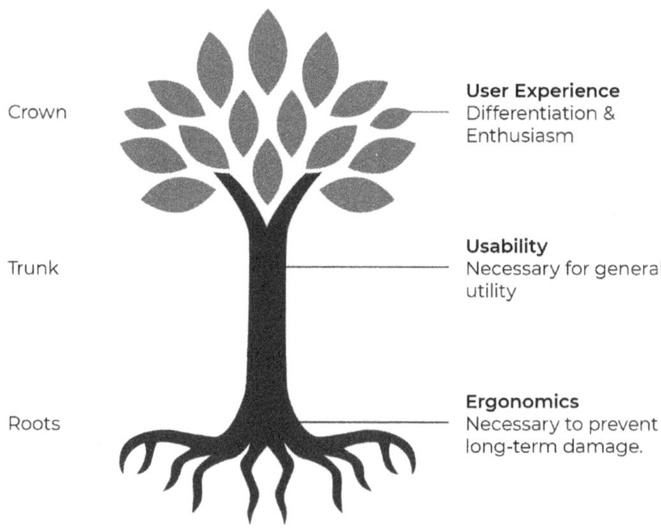

Tree metaphor for ergonomics, usability, and user experience (Franz & Kauer-Franz 2024[33]).

As we have seen, in our view, UX is a dynamic interplay of ergonomics, usability, and emotional engagement, creating experiences that are not only functional but also inspiring. This aligns perfectly with all the aspects we have heard so far. The tree is just a metaphor we use to explain this interplay to new students. However, understanding what makes great UX is only part of the equation. We must measure their impact effectively to improve products and justify UX investments. In the next chapter, our UX Titans will share their insights on measuring UX, prioritizing improvements, and communicating its value to stakeholders. You will learn how they combine data-driven methods with user-centered principles to make a compelling case for UX in every project.

6

Measuring UX and understanding its ROI

Chapter six

Measuring UX and understanding its ROI

6.1 What to expect from this chapter

In this chapter, we will explore the pivotal role of UX measurement in driving user-centered design and delivering business value. UX measurement is not just about collecting data; it is about using it to tell compelling stories, advocate for user needs, and align design decisions with strategic goals.

With the help of our Titans, we will:

- Address the challenges of measuring UX
- Dive into the return on investment of UX
- Uncover strategies for connecting UX efforts to tangible business metrics, demonstrating return on investment.

6.2 The challenges of measuring UX

Measuring UX presents a unique set of challenges that extend beyond numbers and metrics. While tools and frameworks for measurement exist (we'll discuss some in Chapter 7), their application often encounters roadblocks. According to our Titans, these challenges arise from the inherent complexity of user experiences and organizational factors hindering effective measurement practices. Let us dig deeper:

6.2.1 The complexity of UX measurement

User experience encompasses emotions, behaviors, and interactions – not always easily quantified elements. Metrics like satisfaction scores and task completion rates can provide insights, but they fail to capture the nuanced motivations and barriers users face. Marc Hassenzahl highlights this limitation: "I argue for measuring the experience directly, looking at user's emotional needs."

This complexity is further compounded by the need for methodologies that bridge technical and emotional dimensions. Bill Albert elaborates on this challenge: "Measurement often depends on a methodology researchers aren't fully comfortable with, especially when it requires both quantitative skills and a deeper understanding of user emotions."

6.2.2 Organizational and cultural barriers

Another challenge lies within organizations. UX measurement often struggles to gain the support and resources it requires.

Without alignment on the value of measurement, it risks being deprioritized. Dominique Winter points out the common hesitation to research: "Many companies resist investing in robust user research. It's not about the methods – it's about willingness to dedicate time and resources."

This resistance often stems not from a lack of awareness but from insufficient commitment to UX principles. Katja Busch explains: "The problem isn't knowledge; it's commitment and willingness to change. Organizations often hesitate to prioritize user-centric approaches, even when the benefits are clear. User research results can jeopardize the authority to 'own the truth' in a company and thus destabilize the power positions of individual stakeholders."

Without sufficient support for research and iterative processes, UX teams cannot fully realize the value of their efforts. Matthias Schulz reflects on this reality: "Research and iterative approaches are often deprioritized because they are perceived as too costly, even though they save more in the long run."

6.2.3 Linking UX metrics to business goals

One of the most significant challenges is demonstrating how UX impacts business outcomes. While UX improvements often lead to better user satisfaction and engagement, translating these benefits into measurable financial results remains a hurdle. Carmen Fehrenbach points out: "It would be a game-changer to have tools that link UX changes directly to ROI[37] – showing decision-makers the financial impact of better design."

[37] ROI is the shortened version of Return on Investment. ROI is a measurement of how much money is being returned for an investment made.

Matthias Schulz also highlights the importance of framing UX metrics in a business context: "We need metrics that resonate with stakeholders – something tangible, like cost savings or revenue growth, to make UX's value undeniable."

Put the other way around: metrics risk being ignored if they fail to resonate with stakeholders. Thomas Vöhringer-Kuhnt states: "UX metrics must be tied to business goals; otherwise, they risk being ignored by the leadership."

This is also highlighted by Dominique Winter. "It's about delivering value within the limits of an organization's resources. You can create the best possible experience, but it must still be profitable." This balance between user experience and business goals is often overlooked or not appropriately addressed when bringing UX to a company.

6.2.4 Lack of standardized methods

Another challenge is the lack of standardized methods for measuring UX. The result is inconsistency across projects and difficulties in scaling UX practices effectively. This challenge is particularly pronounced in large organizations with diverse teams. Nis Boy Naeve reflects on this challenge: "Scaling UX practices across large organizations is still unresolved, especially when it comes to consistent measurement."

Gabriela Gomes underscores the broader implications of this inconsistency, emphasizing how standardization could enhance UX integration into business processes: "UX needs consistent standards to integrate smoothly into business processes and deliver clear value."

Kevin Liang puts this topic even further. He says even the wording is inconsistent: "We need a shared vocabulary for UX metrics – something that aligns teams and ensures results are actionable."

6.3 What is the ROI of UX?

As we saw in the last section, measuring UX is about understanding users and demonstrating how those insights translate into tangible value for organizations. This topic is critical from our Titan's (and our) perspective, so we dedicated a separate chapter to the return on investment (ROI) of UX.

6.3.1 The elusiveness of ROI

The journey to calculate the ROI of UX often feels like chasing a moving target. Many UX Titans agree that achieving a precise calculation in the traditional sense – a direct financial return for UX investment – is nearly impossible. Dominique Winter refers to it as: "The holy grail because everyone strives for it, but no one ever truly attains it. UX ROI is incredibly hard to calculate because it's holistic and intertwined with other activities."

Bill Albert echoes this challenge, highlighting the complex and interconnected factors: "It's logical but really hard to tie directly. So many things change, and you can't draw a straight line from 'we did this' to 'we made money.'"

As we delve deeper into this topic, it becomes clear that the multidimensional nature of UX, with influences from marketing, competitive shifts, and external circumstances, makes ROI a challenging metric to isolate. However, this complexity doesn't diminish its importance; it requires a different approach.

6.3.2 Alternative ways to frame ROI

If calculating ROI in the traditional sense is elusive, how can we still demonstrate UX's value? The Titans suggest looking beyond numbers to tell a compelling story. Carmen Fehrenbach proposes focusing on qualitative narratives: "Instead of focusing on ROI in a traditional sense, I think showing before-and-after effects or success stories is more effective."

This idea of framing ROI around emotional and experiential outcomes is echoed by Dominique Winter: "Even if I can't calculate ROI in a classic sense, I collect testimonials that highlight emotional responses, like people saying, 'Wow, this is awesome.' That emotional impact can still be framed as a return."

Gabriela Gomes also highlights this broader impact: "When you have good usability, you increase trust with your users, which links directly to success. Good UX removes friction and creates loyalty, which translates to business value."

These alternative approaches emphasize that UX does not always rely on hard financial metrics to prove its value. Through vivid, qualitative evidence of improvement and user satisfaction, stakeholders can often be convinced.

6.3.3 Data as a tool for ROI advocacy

While storytelling and broader metrics help frame ROI, data remains a powerful tool for making ROI arguments tangible and actionable. Oliver Kulpi underscores the need for data-driven discussions: "You can't argue ROI without data. Without it, you're back to gut feelings. Data-driven discussions are what make the case for UX investments."

Matthias Schulz describes a practical method for demonstrating ROI through comparison: "We do before-and-after measurements, using reports with hard data and testimonials from users or stakeholders to show the impact."

When aligned with business goals, data provides a solid foundation for ROI discussions, enabling teams to present measurable outcomes that resonate with decision-makers.

6.3.4 Economic impact on financial metrics

Besides those indirect measures, some Titans advocate for direct financial metrics. Ulf Schubert explains: "Does it reduce costs or increase revenue? UX must support those goals. That's its ROI."

Kerstin Dyck shares one example illustrating the efficiency gains from improved UX in B2B applications: "A better UX can reduce training times for B2B applications, cutting unproductive time and saving costs. That's a straightforward ROI argument."

Thomas Vöhringer-Kuhnt adds another dimension by linking better UX to reduced customer support costs: "If users can complete tasks with fewer support calls, that's a direct cost saving and a clear ROI for UX."

6.4 Summary

This chapter has explored the multifaceted nature of UX measurement and its connection to delivering business value. Besides the challenges of quantifying user experiences, the Titans highlighted the benefits and importance of measuring UX effectively.

Key takeaways include:

- **Understanding UX complexity:** Measuring UX is complex. The metrics applied must capture emotional and behavioral nuances to provide meaningful insights.
- **Overcoming organizational barriers:** Advocating for UX requires commitment, storytelling, and alignment with business goals to become successful.
- **Linking UX to business impact:** Metrics should resonate with stakeholders by tying improvements to cost savings, increased revenue, or other tangible benefits. A definition of the business goals and a strict measurement of these are required to show that UX adds to the business instead of just adding to the costs.
- **Measure ROI directly if possible:** Depending on the product, our Titans shared examples of how to measure ROI directly. Those examples include reduced training times in a B2B context or lowered support costs.
- **Framing ROI creatively if needed:** While traditional ROI calculations may be elusive, alternative methods like user testimonials or increased user trust provide compelling evidence of UX value. Identifying relevant goals and measures upfront is a key activity in measuring the ROI of UX.

The consistent message from the Titans is clear: UX measurement is not a one-size-fits-all practice. It requires a strategic, data-driven, and human-centered approach to capture its value and impact on users and organizations.

6.5 Our thoughts

The voices of the UX Titans underscore a critical truth: measuring UX and understanding its ROI is not merely an analytical challenge but a strategic imperative. While traditional financial metrics often fail to capture the full scope of UX's value, a broader, more integrated perspective can bridge this gap.

In addressing ROI, the Titans highlight a critical point that we echo: UX's value often lies beyond immediate financial gains. The impact of UX is found in strengthened trust, greater loyalty, reduced operational costs, and enhanced brand differentiation. While not always quantifiable, these benefits are pivotal to long-term organizational success.

However, we would like to add to our Titan's statements regarding the ROI of UX. One of the most critical lessons we learned is the early planning of ROI. By defining clear objectives at the project's outset, teams can align their efforts with user needs and business priorities. This forward-thinking approach ensures that UX is recognized as a strategic asset rather than a tactical afterthought.

Another dimension the Titans emphasize, which resonates with us, is the need for diverse metrics tailored to each project's goals. No single metric can fully capture the multifaceted nature of UX impact on business value for every case. Instead, we advocate for planning upfront which kind of impact UX should provide in a specific project on the business side. Those impacts can come from different areas (excerpt is taken from Franz & Kauer-Franz 2024):

- Metrics related to systems, products, or services
    - The proportion of functions used
    - The duration of pauses between interactions
    - The number of completed workflow or purchases
    - The number of jumps and terminations within a workflow
    - The amount of "consumed" content
    - ...
- User- and customer-related measures
    - The proportion of positive mentions in social networks
    - The number of customers acquired
    - The number of positive ratings (e.g., five stars in the App Store)
    - The cost per customer acquired
    - The purchase volume per customer
    - ...
- Service-related metrics
    - The number of calls to the support hotline
    - The duration of hotline calls
    - The number of complaints
    - The number of feature-requests
    - The number of support tickets
    - ...

- Project-related metrics [new]
    - o Time until completion of a development project
    - o Required iterations in the development phase.

If you are interested in more metrics to showcase the ROI of UX, you can download the bonus material of this first *Early Buyer Edition* of UX Titans here: www.uxtitans.com/early-buyer-edition

Planning the ROI upfront and evaluating it later can tell an evident success or failure story, which helps advocate for UX or improve UX processes to ensure better outcomes.

Looking ahead, we see immense potential in the evolving landscape of UX measurement. Emerging tools, such as real-time analytics and emotion tracking, promise to make UX impacts more tangible and actionable. However, the foundation remains the same: a thoughtful, user-centered approach backed by strategic planning and solid organizational alignment.

7

Optimizing UX – mindset and methods

Chapter seven

Optimizing UX – mindset and methods

7.1 What to expect from this chapter

This chapter will explore the mindset that powers exceptional UX design. We will discover the foundational principles UXers need to succeed and enable them to connect with users and craft meaningful, resonant designs.

Building on the foundation of the last chapter, we'll uncover some practical methods that form the backbone of great UX work next. You will learn which tools and techniques deliver the most value in the eyes of our Titans and how to avoid the pitfalls of overrated methodologies. With these insights, you will be equipped to optimize UX with confidence and focus.

7.2 The right mindset to optimize UX

Every successful UX professional operates with a mindset attuned to users, their needs, and the dynamic design environment. Let us look at the essential qualities for navigating the complexities of the field.

7.2.1 Curiosity: The heartbeat of UX

Curiosity is repeatedly emphasized as the bedrock of UX success. As Kerstin Dyck explains, "Curiosity is very important for asking questions. Because when I interview, I ask completely different questions if I really want to know the answers." For her, a successful UX designer dives deeply into questions about users, products, and processes, understanding that every detail might hold the key to a solution. This investigative mindset transforms the mundane into an endless source of insight and inspiration.

Uwe Betzin links curiosity to a deeper understanding of human experience. Inspired by the constructivist philosophy of Paul Watzlawick, Uwe believes that every person "acts optimally according to their subjective reality," an idea that fuels his drive to understand user behavior. This notion reframes UX from being about "right" or "wrong" solutions and instead becomes about empathy and immersing oneself in the unique worldview of the user to design meaningful experiences. He adds: "If we understand that every individual has their reality, then it becomes much easier to explore it with curiosity."

7.2.2 Empathy: Building bridges, not just interfaces

Empathy in UX is more than a buzzword; it is the lens through which designers view problems and users. Bill Albert emphasizes that "you have to have empathy for the customer and user," grounding the design process in genuinely understanding people's needs and frustrations.

Marc Hassenzahl describes empathy as "seeing beyond the obvious." For example, when designing a robotic lawnmower interface, he shifts the focus from "How should people operate this?" to a more human-centric "How do we want to mow the lawn?" This perspective prioritizes the user's experience and needs rather than forcing a pre-made solution onto them. Such an "empathy mindset" is helpful for users and indispensable for cross-functional teamwork, as designers collaborate with individuals from various backgrounds, each with their perspectives and constraints.

7.2.3 Humility and adaptability: Letting go to grow

UX is rarely straightforward. The field's iterative nature demands humility, a tolerance for failure, and a willingness to embrace it as a stepping stone to success. Kerstin Dyck vividly illustrates this by describing how designers must be ready to "let go of ideas," even those close to their hearts, when testing shows they do not work. "You have to be able to adapt and say: 'It was a nice idea, but we need to pivot.'"

Kevin Liang echoes this, noting that humility goes hand-in-hand with adaptability. His experience suggests that "UX professionals are too attached to their initial ideas or solutions and often miss valuable opportunities to learn from feedback." For Kevin, humility is a personal asset and a professional necessity, making UXers approachable and effective collaborators who avoid assumptions and focus on data.

Gabriela Gomes adds that humility and adaptability are essential for avoiding burnout. "You need to be flexible and receptive to change because UX is a chaotic process." This chaotic nature, she explains, can lead to "frustration if a designer is not mentally prepared to adapt constantly." This attitude makes UX professionals resilient despite ever-evolving user needs and technical challenges.

7.2.4 Proactivity: A team-user-centric approach

Successful UX professionals do not operate in silos. As Uwe Betzin explains, "UX is a (team) tool in the service of the product." Ulf Schubert adds: "UX fails when it operates in silos. Collaboration across teams is essential." The perspective of seeing UX as a tool used in teams empowers you to think about your role and the team itself proactively. He continues: "It's up to me to teach them...how I contribute to the product."

Matthias Schulz builds on this, noting that "UX leaders must cultivate an enabling environment for their team." A good UX manager understands the evolving needs of users, the team, and the company, constantly evaluating whether current approaches fit. For Matthias, a "UX leader's role is not to control every detail but to strengthen the team by fostering a culture of continuous learning and adaptation."

7.3 The best methods to optimize UX

In the last chapter, we've already discussed the Titan's view on measuring UX on a high level. We want to dig deeper into specific methods and their combination within this section.

7.3.1 The power of qualitative methods

Many Titans choose qualitative methods as their primary tool. Those methods include UX testing, field observation, diary studies, and thinking aloud.

Uwe Betzin emphasizes the importance of engaging directly with end users through UX tests in each sprint cycle. In his approach, testing is not just a routine but a vital part of the development cycle that continuously informs what gets built next. He explains: "End-user sessions are key. These sessions allow me to test what's been developed and identify what we need to learn. With them, we'd retain that critical feedback loop. And if it's one method I'd rely on, it would be moderated, qualitative sessions. They're time-consuming but bring the most results."

Similarly, UX Testing is Carmen Fehrenbach's preferred method for getting insights beyond numbers on a page: "Quantitative stuff is nice, but it often ends up forgotten. UX tests, though? They let us refine new concepts and understand things better. That's never boring."

In addition, field observation allows researchers to see firsthand how users interact with products in natural environments, helping UX professionals uncover the unspoken needs and pain points that might go unnoticed in controlled settings. Gert-Dieter Tuzar considers observation foundational: "Observation is the core of all scientific methods. Watching users in the field, seeing how they solve problems or struggle, reveals so much more than any figures can."

7.3.2 Blending observation with rapid iteration

Several UX Titans advocate for a method that balances observation with rapid iteration, such as the RITE (Rapid Iterative Testing and Evaluation) method. Gabriela Gomes highlights the unique advantage of this approach: "RITE lets us catch usability issues early and fix them fast. Originally developed for games like Age of Empires II, it allows for continuous improvement through multiple rounds of quick testing. The earlier you fail and test your assumptions, the better."

By combining observational insights with quick adjustments, the RITE method fosters an agile development cycle that identifies and addresses issues in real-time.

7.3.3 Positive experience patterns

Some experts, like Marc Hassenzahl, focus on identifying and replicating positive user experiences rather than fixing usability problems. His unique approach, Experience Pattern Analysis, captures moments when users genuinely enjoy a product or service: "Rather than asking users what they dislike, we focus on what they love. When did they enjoy a train journey, for instance? Understanding these positive moments lets us create experiences that others can enjoy."

7.3.4 Diary studies: Real-world insights over time

Diary studies offer a versatile solution for UX researchers looking to capture long-term, real-world insights. Kevin Liang is a strong advocate of this approach, which involves users documenting their experiences over time:

"Diary studies, or ecological momentary assessment, let us capture user needs as they happen. It's flexible and helps us see real-life patterns across different situations and times." This method captures how users' needs and reactions evolve, providing a fuller picture of their interaction with a product or service.

7.3.5 Quick and dirty: The coffee kitchen test

For some UX Titans, quick, informal feedback is sometimes as valuable as a formal test. Thomas Vöhriger-Kuhnt uses an approach he calls "Coffee Kitchen Usability Testing," where he gathers rapid feedback on prototypes in casual settings, such as by asking coworkers in the break room: "Quick and dirty testing, grabbing a few colleagues in the coffee kitchen to test early-stage wireframes, can be incredibly revealing. It's not formal and does not replace user testing, but it lets us get feedback early."

7.3.6 Hybrid approaches: Merging quantitative and qualitative insights

Although the Titans mainly focus on qualitative methods, some prefer a mixed approach. Bill Albert, for instance, prefers an approach that merges qualitative observations with quantitative data. Combining these elements, he seeks a balance of depth and scale: "I need qual and quant together, like a soft-serve chocolate and vanilla twist. Pure surveys need more depth, while interviews are too few to quantify trends. But field intercepts – quick, on-the-go studies with large groups – give me a mix of measurement and insight. That's my ice cream cone."

Marc Hassenzahl also stresses the value of a balanced approach, cautioning against over-reliance on any single method: "Relying solely on metrics risks fetishizing numbers. Combining quantitative data with qualitative insights gives us a fuller picture of the experience."

7.4 The most overrated methods to optimize UX

In the previous sections, we explored methods that consistently yield impactful results. In this chapter, we'll focus on methods that, while valuable in specific contexts, are often misapplied or overused. From tools like eye-tracking to personas, we'll examine why our UX Titans see these approaches sometimes fail to deliver on their promise and how to ensure they're used effectively.

7.4.1 Eye-Tracking: The heatmap hype

According to some of our Titans, eye-tracking is the poster child of overrated UX methodologies. Its colorful heatmaps and scientific appeal have long made it a darling of stakeholders seeking quantifiable results. Yet, many UX professionals question its actual utility in the context of cost and practicality. Dominique Winter illustrates this skepticism vividly: "Eye-tracking is completely overrated. It's like doing a think-aloud test with 200 people when you're supposed to solve the most important issues with just five. Most products aren't mature enough to even need it yet."

Similarly, Sarah Diefenbach highlights the method's tendency to impress without delivering actionable insights: "You get these nice, colorful heatmaps, but they don't tell you much. What's missing is the 'why.' Interviews or observations would add more value." Thomas Vöhringer-Kuhnt agrees: "You know that a user is looking at one place more than another. What does that tell me? It's just very expensive, and the gain in knowledge is not in proportion to the effort."

Ulf Schubert provides a pragmatic perspective, emphasizing the impracticality of small sample sizes: "When you do eye-tracking with 15 people, you can't read much from it. To do it right is ultra-expensive, and most of us don't have that time or budget."

7.4.2 Physiological data: The "nice to have" that rarely delivers

Beyond eye-tracking, other physiological methods like EEG, skin conductivity, and face-reading tools are often deemed extravagant for practical UX work. These techniques demand significant resources and deliver insights that rarely justify the investment.

Thomas Vöhringer-Kuhnt succinctly captures the frustration: "Like eye-tracking, the knowledge gain is not proportional to the effort. The results may look cool, but what do they really tell me? It's just not worth it."

Matthias Schulz echoes this sentiment, pointing to the gulf between academic applications and real-world utility: "In science, where you take time for detailed analysis, these methods work. In practice, where we do not have the time to analyze one measure for a week, they don't. Most products aren't emotionally charged enough to benefit from such data."

7.4.3 Personas: The trap of stereotyping

Personas have become a staple of UX design, yet some Titans argue that their oversimplification often limits innovation. Gert-Dieter Tuzar critiques the narrow focus they can impose: "You're designing for a persona who's a caricature – a penthouse-dwelling millionaire who doesn't represent the broader audience. It's too limiting."

Similarly, Lutz Krauß recalls early projects where personas veered into absurdity: "We'd create in former times personas like 'Top Gun' or 'Soccer Mom,' and they felt more like marketing trophies than tools for meaningful design."

7.4.4 Quantitative overreliance: Numbers without nuances

Quantitative methods, such as surveys and A/B testing, are invaluable but can quickly become counterproductive when misused. Tobias Oberpaul explains, "A/B testing can tell you which version performs better, but not why. Without a clear hypothesis, it becomes a time-consuming and costly guessing game."

Surveys, often chosen for their speed and scale, face similar criticism. Kevin Liang highlights their potential for misuse: "Surveys are the easiest method to deploy and the hardest to get right. Without careful design, they often produce more misleading than helpful results."

7.4.5 Other overrated methods that were mentioned by only one Titan

While some methods are broadly considered overrated by multiple UX Titans, others were singled out by individual experts for their shortcomings. Though less frequently discussed, these methods highlight nuances in UX practice where certain tools or approaches might not deliver the expected value. Below are the methods mentioned by individual Titans:

- **High-fidelity prototypes:** Nis Boy Naeve laments the undue emphasis placed on them: "High-fidelity prototypes take time and don't always add value. Yet, stakeholders demand them for the 'wow' factor, even when simpler approaches would suffice."
- **Card Sorting:** Carmen Fehrenbach notes the limited value of card sorting for significant design insights: "I've had few 'aha' moments with card sorting. It's often time-consuming without transformative results".
- **Extreme focus on visual consistency with corporate standards:** It's not a method but a common practice. Katja Busch critiques excessive attention to aligning designs

with corporate visual standards at the expense of usability: "Too much focus on brand design can overshadow usability and cognitive psychology principles."

7.4.6 Final thoughts: Every tool has its place

Despite their criticisms, none of the UX Titans outright dismiss the methods mentioned. As Nis Boy Naeve explains, "The main thing is to start somewhere. Any method is better than no method if it brings UX to the table". This highlights the importance of using methods thoughtfully rather than avoiding them entirely.

The key takeaway? While all UX methods may have flaws, the real challenge lies in over-reliance or misuse. Bill Albert illustrates this point with usability testing: "It's great and used all the time, but it's overused when small sample sizes are used for preference-based questions. Usability testing isn't designed to tell you what six out of ten people like; it's about uncovering usability issues. Misusing it this way leads to unreliable conclusions".

The consistent message from the Titans is that no tool is inherently ineffective. Success lies in understanding a method's strengths, limitations, and the context in which it's applied.

7.5 Summary

In this chapter, we've explored the mindset and methods that form the foundation of exceptional UX design. Through the voices of our UX Titans, we've learned the following key lessons:

- **Mindset - The core of UX success:** The success of UX professionals lies in their mindset. Curiosity drives a deeper understanding of user behaviors and needs. Empathy allows designers to step into users' shoes and prioritize meaningful experiences. Humility and adaptability enable UXers to embrace change, pivot ideas, and grow through iteration. Finally, proactivity empowers UXers to act as bridges between teams and users, fostering a collaborative, user-centric culture. These qualities create a foundation for impactful design, aligning user needs with business goals.
- **Methods - A balanced toolkit:** Our UX Titans favor practical, qualitative methods as the cornerstone of effective UX work. Techniques like field studies, diary studies, and iterative testing enable teams to uncover authentic insights and make rapid improvements. Hybrid approaches that combine qualitative depth with quantitative scale provide a fuller picture of user needs.
- **Overrated methods – or every tool has its place:** No UX method is inherently ineffective, but some are widely used with a false focus. Eye tracking, for example, can be compelling but is often overused without clear goals or sufficient sample sizes. Similarly, personas risk

oversimplification when not grounded in robust research. The consistent message from our Titans is clear: Success lies in understanding the strengths and limitations of each tool and applying them thoughtfully.

7.6 Our thoughts

As we reflect on the statements of our Titans in this chapter, they align very well with our insights. One of the most essential qualities of a UXer is their mindset. It is critical to the success of any UX effort.

If we had to describe the required mindset, we would use words similar to those already used by our Titans. However, we would like to add another component: try to show that your user interface / UX is NOT good.

What do we mean by that? Imagine a team designing a product. While working on the product, they make many assumptions about the user. To fulfill the user's needs, the team puts in tremendous effort and crafts a compelling UX (at least in their opinion). When it comes to user testing, the team hopes to get good results. They want to show (at least subconsciously) that they have done a great job and the UX is fantastic. That is relatable, but in our opinion, it is the wrong approach. It too often leads to downplaying and neglecting real usability problems.

Imagine the same team with a shift in their approach. When it comes to user testing, they now would like to show that the UX is not good. This focus makes it much easier to uncover the problems. It leads to much less downplaying and allows faster improvements.

In the next chapter, we asked: What is the best way to start and do UX in an organization? Let's see what our Titans answered.

8

Starting UX in the company – the UX revolution begins

Chapter eight

Starting UX in the company – the UX revolution begins

8.1 What to expect from this chapter

Embarking on introducing UX into a company is both a challenge and an opportunity. In this chapter, you will learn why UX is a cornerstone of modern business success and how to navigate the complexities of embedding it into your organization. We will explore strategies to overcome resistance, leverage small wins, and gain the support needed to make UX a sustainable and transformative part of your company's culture. Drawing from the wisdom of our Titans, this chapter serves as a practical guide to building a foundation for UX that thrives.

8.2 Why start UX in your company?

UX is not just a discipline; the heart of a user-centered approach differentiates great companies from merely good ones. As Gert-

Dieter Tuzar puts it: "Whenever you create something for people, you need to ask yourself: Are you not only doing it successfully but also doing it the right way?". Every interaction with a product, service, or interface is an opportunity to delight users and forge lasting connections. Thomas Vöhringer-Kuhnt discusses UX similarly, calling it "a long-term customer loyalty program."

For Kevin Liang, the essence of UX is directly tied to the health of a business: "Companies exist to solve problems for people; if you neglect their experience, you lose your business." This is echoed by Marc Hassenzahl, who argues, "As soon as your company interacts with people, investing in UX becomes a necessity." Or as Bill Albert puts it, "If a company has users or customers, they must invest in UX to create better experiences."

Ulf Schubert gives another argument for starting UX in companies: differentiation. He says: "Differentiating through experience is vital in competitive markets where technical advantages are short-lived." He continues: "Even when technical advantages are big, experiences matter nevertheless."

8.3 Steps to start UX in a company

How do you transform the idea of UX into action? While the path may seem daunting, taking deliberate, strategic steps can make all the difference. In this section, we will uncover the most effective ways to introduce UX, using the lessons learned from those who have already succeeded.

8.3.1 What's your why? Unlocking the purpose of UX

Before diving into UX, ask yourself: Why does your company need UX? Without a clear purpose, efforts risk becoming scattered and ineffective. "Start with identifying the problems UX will solve for both the company and the users or customers. It's not a department - it's a mindset and process," says Katja Busch.

Every company's starting point is different. As Uwe Betzin notes, "Understand your company's current approach to user interactions before introducing UX." This clarity allows you to align UX with user needs and business objectives.

Practical actions:

- **Align with business goals directly from the start:** We have already discussed this topic in Chapter 6. But since this is the guide to start, we need to discuss it again: "UX thrives when it's tied to measurable outcomes that resonate with leadership," says Gert-Dieter Tuzar. Dominique Winter agrees: "When UX aligns with broader company goals, it becomes easier to gain support."
- **Define what success is:** Whether it is increasing Net Promoter Scores or improving usability ratings, ensure goals are quantifiable and set. "Defining success upfront keeps teams focused and accountable," suggests Ulf Schubert.
- **Document the "Before":** To show the success of UX later, it is vital to document how the metrics and user interfaces were before.

8.3.2 How do you make UX visible? Building awareness that sticks

Creating awareness is the next step in winning support for UX. But how do you make people care about something they might not fully understand? Here are the steps our Titans suggest:

Practical actions:

- **Host workshops and training:** "Regular workshops demystify UX and build confidence in its methods," suggests Guido Meier-Arendt. While doing so, "Articulate the value of UX and tailor your message to the company's specific challenges and goals," advises Gabriela Gomes.
- **Share case studies from others:** Highlight examples of UX success within your industry. "Success stories inspire belief in UX's potential. Even if they are not your own stories yet." Carmen Fehrenbach notes.

8.3.3 Can small wins lead to big changes? Start with pilot projects, but don't call them UX.

To get the first wins, pilot projects are your secret weapon. They allow you to experiment, showcase success, and build momentum without committing significant resources. " Pilot projects allow teams to see UX benefits fast and firsthand," says Kerstin Dyck.

Kevin Liang advises, "Do a small project, show results, but avoid calling it 'UX.' Let the success speak for itself." Early wins create trust and pave the way for more significant initiatives.

Practical actions:

- **Select a manageable project:** Choose a project with clear goals and measurable outcomes. "Small, focused projects demonstrate value more effectively than broad, vague efforts," suggests Oliver Kulpi. Ulf Schubert advises: "Prioritize areas where UX can drive the most significant improvement for the user and the business."
- **Involve open-minded teams:** Work with teams willing to experiment and innovate. "Collaborating with early adopters can build enthusiasm and credibility," says Guido Meier-Arendt.
- **Show measurable results:** Highlight outcomes on the previously defined (business) metrics. "Quantifiable success stories inspire others to follow suit," explains Gert-Dieter Tuzar. Carmen Fehrenbach adds: "Success stories, especially those with measurable outcomes, inspire buy-in across the company."

8.3.4 Who's on your side? Finding allies across teams

Success in UX depends on more than tools and techniques – it requires people who believe in its value. The next step is to "build on the first wins and find the critical mass," Nis Boy Naeve emphasizes. Building these relationships strengthens your foundation and amplifies advocacy efforts.

Practical actions:

- **Identify more enthusiastic individuals/teams:** Seek out more people in different departments who see the value of UX. "Building cross-functional support creates a ripple effect," says Kevin Liang.
- **Create collaboration opportunities:** Encourage interaction between those individuals/teams through workshops or collaborative projects. These collaborative efforts lead to faster adoption. "Collaborative spaces allow for shared learning and alignment," advises Kerstin Dyck.
- **Grow collaboration into a UX community:** Form a working group or community of practice. "Internal networks keep UX momentum alive and encourage knowledge sharing," notes Guido Meier-Arendt.

8.3.5 How do you win over leaders? Securing executive buy-in

After finding allies across teams, winning leaders for your side is essential. Without executive buy-in, UX initiatives risk being overlooked or underfunded. This step can be straightforward since we have already tied UX goals with business goals. Of course, it does not have to be...

Practical actions:

- **Show your UX results (which align with business goals) often:** This seems trivial but is often overlooked in practice. Show how UX improves revenue, reduces costs, or enhances customer loyalty. "Leadership cares about results – connect UX to their priorities," advises Gert-Dieter Tuzar.

- **Involve leaders in UX activities:** Invite them to observe user research, such as usability tests. "Seeing UX in action builds empathy and advocacy. Stakeholders who experience UX firsthand are more likely to become advocates." says Kevin Liang.
- **Present the before-and-after comparison:** In an early step, our Titans suggested documenting the before. Now, it is time to use it to present the ROI of UX. "A clear before-and-after comparison is hard to ignore," notes Gabriela Gomes.

The first steps in introducing UX – defining its purpose, creating awareness, achieving small wins, and securing buy-in – lay the groundwork for its success. But how do you transform these initial victories into a sustained organizational shift?

8.4 Building a long-term UX culture

Scaling up UX requires more than repeating early successes. It involves embedding UX into your company's DNA, ensuring it becomes a fundamental part of how teams operate and make decisions. Let us find out how our Titans would proceed.

8.4.1 How do you scale UX?

Scaling UX is about broadening its influence beyond isolated teams or projects. To achieve this, organizations must create systems that make UX accessible and actionable for everyone.

Practical actions:

- **Develop standardized frameworks:** Reuse by creating and using design systems, toolkits, and templates. "Shared frameworks make UX practices scalable and ensure consistency across teams," says Kerstin Dyck.
- **Empower even more cross-functional collaboration:** Encourage departments like product, marketing, and engineering to incorporate UX into their workflows. "Collaboration across roles ensures UX is embedded in daily work," advises Guido Meier-Arendt. Tobias Oberpaul adds: "A single passionate individual can plant the seeds of UX in startups, but larger organizations need more."
- **Create centers of excellence:** Establish a centralized UX team to provide expertise and guidance. "A strong central team can train others and drive consistent standards," notes Oliver Kulpi.
- **Be patient - cultural change is hard:** When scaling UX, it becomes clear that changing a culture is hard work and takes time. As Gert-Dieter Tuzar explains, "Cultural change is gradual and requires evolutionary, not revolutionary, approaches."

8.4.2 Embedding UX in processes: Making it non-negotiable

To ensure UX thrives long-term, it must be integrated into the organization's processes, from ideation to delivery. Without structural support, efforts risk being inconsistent or dependent on specific individuals.

Practical actions:

- **Incorporate UX into decision gates:** Require UX validation at key project milestones. "UX must influence decisions to ensure user needs are considered," says Ulf Schubert.
- **Establish governance:** Create policies to standardize UX practices and ensure accountability. "Governance ensures consistency and prevents backsliding," advises Ulf Schubert.
- **Align UX with business strategy:** Tie UX goals directly to organizational objectives. "Embedding UX into the company strategy makes it indispensable," explains Katja Busch.

8.4.3 Sustaining the culture: Fostering a UX mindset.

Scaling up UX is also about developing a culture where user-centricity is second nature. This requires ongoing education, reinforcement, and leadership support.

Practical actions:

- **Educate continuously:** Provide regular training and onboarding sessions to ensure new and existing employees understand UX principles. "Ongoing education keeps UX alive in the organization," says Uwe Betzin. This could be done through the already suggested central UX team.
- **Promote UX champions:** Recognize and support employees who advocate for UX. "Building a network of champions strengthens UX's influence across teams," notes Nis Boy Naeve.
- **Lead by example:** Ensure leadership visibly supports and prioritizes UX. "Leaders must live user-centricity to inspire others," advises Dominique Winter.

8.4.4 How do you handle growing pains? Navigating challenges at scale

As UX scales, new challenges emerge from resource constraints to maintaining quality across larger teams. Addressing these growing pains is critical to sustaining momentum.

Practical actions:

- **Prioritize staffing:** Ensure teams have enough UX professionals to meet demand. "A balance of skills and resources is key to scaling effectively," says Tobias Oberpaul.

- **Monitor and measure:** Keep using UX (business) metrics to track progress and identify areas for improvement. "Governance must include measurable outcomes to ensure accountability," advises Ulf Schubert.
- **Adapt and evolve:** Stay open to refining processes and frameworks as the organization grows. "Scaling UX is an iterative process that requires flexibility," says Oliver Kulpi.

8.5 Summary

Introducing and scaling UX in a company is a transformative journey that requires patience, persistence, and strategic action. It begins with a clear purpose – defining why UX matters for your organization and aligning it with business goals. Early wins, such as pilot projects and stakeholder engagement, demonstrate value and build trust, paving the way for broader adoption.

Challenges like resistance to change, limited resources, and team misalignment are inevitable but surmountable. By fostering collaboration, sharing compelling success stories, and securing executive buy-in, UX can evolve from isolated efforts into a unifying force within the organization.

To ensure UX thrives long-term, it must be embedded into processes, scaled across teams, and championed at every level. Governance, continuous education, and a user-centric culture are essential to sustaining its impact.

The path to a UX-driven culture is challenging but leads to transformative results for users, teams, and the business.

Success lies in building momentum, staying adaptable, and never losing sight of the ultimate goal: creating meaningful experiences that resonate.

Remember: In the bonus material of this *Early Buyer Edition* of UX Titans, there is a cheat sheet for starting UX in your company based on this chapter. You can download it here: www.uxtitans.com/early-buyer-edition

8.6 Our thoughts

Reflecting on our Titans answers, we realized that our UX experience comes from supporting product development companies with UX services. As a result, we have seen many different cultures, products, and approaches to UX.

They all have in common that UX is given a high enough priority. They would not work with an external UX agency if this were not the case. However, we saw a lot of "first tries" – companies who tried to do UX for the first time.

UX is considered a huge effort for those companies, at least in the past. The same is true for companies who do not do UX at all. In many cases, UX seems to be an add-on.

Let us explain: Let us say you develop software. What do you need to do to make the software a saleable product? If you answer this question, you will probably come up with topics such as programming, marketing, and sales. Perhaps customer service will be added. Rarely does anyone mention "UX" as a minimum component. And that is the problem: UX is often considered a nice-to-have.

But this abruptly changes when you show the power of UX. Our Titans suggest, among other things, linking it to business goals. In our view, this is the top step. If you succeed in this step, it is often very easy to convince stakeholders, or they are already convinced.

We want to highlight another suggestion, already mentioned by Kevin Liang, that has proven successful in our practice: Get a budget stakeholder to participate in a full UX test. We already highlighted the typical first test experience from "stupid user" over "we have a problem" to "how could we ever have worked differently" in Chapter 2.5. In other words, we have witnessed the creation of a new UX advocate multiple times. This is the strongest argument for UX: observing your users with your product.

9

The perfect UX team

Chapter nine

The perfect UX team

9.1 What to expect from this chapter

What does it take to build a great UX team? This chapter delves into the essential elements of creating a team that drives innovation and delivers outstanding user experiences.

We explore why you need a team, what makes an ideal team structure, and how to identify and attract top talent. You will also learn practical strategies for fostering a culture that inspires retention, creativity, and continuous growth. Through insights from the Titans, we uncover the critical factors contributing to a thriving UX team, from collaboration across disciplines to purpose-driven leadership.

9.2 Do you even need a team?

We've already discussed in Chapter 7.2.4 that a UX team is vital for our Titans.

However, organizations often struggle with whether they need a team or a solo UXer, especially in the early stages of integrating UX into their workflows. While the idea of a lone UXer handling every aspect might sound efficient, the reality is far more complex.

9.2.1 The myth of the lone UX unicorn

The myth of the lone UXer is one of self-sufficiency, brilliance, and endless creativity. Uwe Betzin humorously puts it: "As a magical unicorn, I ride over the product, leave fairy dust behind, and everything is beautiful. No, [UX] is a team sport, of course (laughs). It's a must; UX can't be done alone. UX is also too important to leave it to the designers."

While some solo UXers might manage, the reality is often much more challenging. Matthias Schulz shares: "A solo UXer might survive if they can access a supportive community, but it's a lonely road. Without collaboration, a burnout or stagnation is inevitable." The sheer breadth of UX work – from research to design, from user testing to stakeholder communication – can overwhelm even the most talented individual. UX can be a solo endeavor under certain conditions, but this is always a suboptimal solution. Most Titans agree that UX is too complex for one person to handle all its facets effectively.

9.2.2 Why UX is the ultimate team sport

This is one of the parts on which ALL UX Titans agree: Great UX work thrives on collaboration and blending diverse perspectives. Bill Albert explains: "Within the team, we have researchers, designers, product managers, and business analysts. Everyone has a different perspective, and bringing them together is essential."

The reason teamwork is so crucial lies in the multidisciplinary nature of UX. Combining creative problem-solving with technical feasibility and business strategy requires input from multiple disciplines. Marc Hassenzahl emphasizes, "You need someone creative, someone conceptual, and someone technical. Add social scientists who understand people and groups; suddenly, you have a multidimensional team capable of addressing almost any challenge."

Finally, the dynamic exchange within teams often leads to solutions that no person could have envisioned alone. As Gabriela Gomes notes, "The best work I've seen is when designers collaborate closely with engineers or other relevant disciplines. We're not just working on the product's user experience but creating an environment where everyone's expertise is valued."

Together, these perspectives illustrate why UX is a field that demands collaboration to succeed. When teams come together, they multiply their impact, driving richer, more effective solutions that deliver true value to users and businesses alike.

9.3 What does the perfect team look like?

According to Katja Busch, building a UX team is like casting in a heist movie: "The size and structure of a UX team depend on the task. It's like casting for Ocean's Eleven – each member is chosen for their expertise." But where would our Titans start? And who would they choose? Let us find out!

9.3.1 Mission impossible? Defining the core of a UX team

At its heart, every UX team needs a solid foundation of core skills and roles. As Gert-Dieter Tuzar explains, "An effective team needs different roles. The composition depends on the objectives." Building on different roles ensures that the team can address every stage of the UX process, from understanding users to implementing designs.

While the exact mix often varies, some roles are universally important:

- **Business Strategists:** To align the UX efforts with organizational goals.
- **User Researchers:** To uncover user needs and insights.
- **UX Designers:** To translate insights into usable and appealing designs.
- **Developers:** To bring designs to life through technical implementation.

Each role is essential, and their collaboration ensures the team can tackle challenges from multiple angles.

9.3.2 Teamwork in action: Fostering collaboration across roles

Having the right roles in place is good, but only half the battle – teams thrive when there is a true collaboration. Tobias Oberpaul stresses the importance of cross-disciplinary understanding:

"Each role should understand the perspectives of the others – developers must grasp UX, and UXers need to understand business constraints." This shared understanding creates a more unified team capable of delivering technically feasible, user-centered solutions aligned with business needs.

Additionally, Katja Busch highlights, "The perfect team is transparent, empathetic, and willing to support one another. Team alignment matters more than individual skill."

9.3.3 Scaling the mountain: Adaptability as a key characteristic

No two projects or organizations are the same, and UX teams must be adaptable to succeed. Guido Meier-Ahrendt says, "Some projects require smaller teams, while others may need extensive collaboration across departments." In some projects, a small and agile team might be best. In other environments, a larger cross-functional team could be ideal.

Additionally, according to our Titans, adaptability extends beyond size. Teams may need to evolve as projects progress, such as adding researchers during discovery phases or adding more developers during implementation. This ability to scale and pivot ensures the team remains effective, regardless of the challenges ahead. Therefore, adaptability is a key characteristic of an outstanding UX team.

9.3.4 The secret sauce: A team culture that thrives

Katja Busch already highlighted that transparency, empathy, and supporting each other are more important than individual skills. Other Titans agree: Great UX teams are not just about skills. They have a great team culture. As Ulf Schubert shares, "Empathy, fairness, and a focus on shared goals drive UX teams to success. Culture is key."

A thriving culture also includes openness to feedback and a willingness to grow. This creates an environment where team members feel empowered to contribute their best work, knowing their voices are valued.

9.4 Building and maintaining a great UX team

Now that we know what the perfect team looks like according to our Titans, let us find out how they would build and sustain it. This section explores how to identify the best UX professionals, bring them on board, and create an environment where they can grow and succeed.

9.4.1 Finding the gems: How to recognize top UX talent

The best UX professionals share certain traits that make them stand out. Bill Albert highlights three critical qualities: "Great UXers are curious, adaptable, and excellent problem-solvers." Curiosity drives them to ask the right questions and explore innovative solutions, while adaptability helps them navigate the ever-changing landscape of user needs and business goals.

As we already saw, empathy is another defining characteristic. Marc Hassenzahl emphasizes its importance: "Empathy and the ability to switch perspectives are essential traits for UXers. Great UXers understand users and connect with team members and stakeholders, making collaboration more effective."

Katja Busch adds that critical thinking is just as vital: "The ability to analyze problems critically, combined with empathy and intelligence, defines great UX professionals." Combining emotional and analytical skills enables UXers to tackle complex challenges and create meaningful solutions.

When evaluating candidates, look beyond their technical skills to assess how they approach problems, communicate ideas, and collaborate with others. Practical exercises, portfolio reviews, and in-depth discussions can reveal these qualities.

9.4.2 Winning hearts: Attracting UX talent that fits

Recognizing great talent is one crucial step. Additionally, you need to attract your dream UXers to your team. Kevin Liang explains the importance of authenticity: "You must exemplify your team's values and create an authentic recruitment process. Transparency is key." A genuine representation of your culture helps candidates to see if they align with your organization's vision.

Kerstin Dyck underscores the role of an appealing work environment: "The company culture must be appealing, with flexibility, inclusivity, and opportunities for growth." UX professionals are often drawn to organizations that offer work-life balance and a sense of belonging.

Beyond culture, purpose attracts top talent. Bill Albert notes, "Top UXers thrive when they feel their work has purpose and impact. They want to know their contributions matter – not just to the company but also to the users they serve." Communicating how your team makes a difference can be a powerful draw.

9.4.3 Keeping the spark alive: Retaining and growing your team

Bringing great people into your team is significant, but retaining them is just as important. Dominique Winter highlights the value of feedback and growth opportunities: "Retaining great UXers requires continuous feedback, opportunities for learning, and recognition of their contributions." Regular check-ins and clear pathways for development help keep team members motivated and engaged.

A strong sense of purpose also fosters loyalty. Uwe Betzin explains, "A supportive environment where teams can align their passion with business goals is vital." Bill Albert adds: "Purpose-driven companies attract the best talent and foster long-term engagement."

So, to build and maintain a team of the best UXers, your organization must create an environment where they feel valued and supported.

9.5 Summary

Our Titans believe collaboration is the cornerstone of UX and transforms individual efforts into meaningful, user-centered outcomes. As explored in this chapter, the perfect UX team is built on a diversity – of skills, perspectives, and roles. By blending technical, creative, and strategic expertise, UX teams can tackle complex challenges with a unified vision.

A great UX team does not come together by chance. It requires thoughtful planning and continuous effort. Recognizing, attracting, and retaining top talent are interconnected steps that demand attention and care. From spotting the curiosity and empathy of promising professionals to creating an environment where they can thrive, each part of the process contributes to building a team that excels.

When all these elements come together, a UX team becomes more than just a group of individuals – it transforms into a powerful collaboration machine capable of delivering exceptional results for users and organizations.

Remember: If you are preparing to hire new team members or applying for a job, there is a list of questions you could ask/use to prepare in the bonus material of this *Early Buyer Edition* of UX Titans. You can download it here: www.uxtitans.com/early-buyer-edition

9.6 Our thoughts

Our view of the perfect UX team is partly the same and different. Why is that? As a UX agency, we work in a constellation rarely mentioned in the interviews with our Titans. As an agency, we are outsiders and can only be part of the client's UX team to a certain extent. As a result, we have different requirements for our UX experts. Three examples:

- We often find ourselves working independently with different teams in large companies. In this constellation, it frequently happens that a team asks us to solve a UX problem that was already solved by another team in the same company for a different product. This exchange happens through external partners like us, especially with no internal UX-sharing structure. Therefore, our UX specialists must recognize and communicate the patterns to help across teams.
- As outsiders, we often do not know why a decision was made that way. Therefore, we often approach a testing situation with a much more open mind and bring to light problems that have already been ticked off internally as "we'll leave it like that." In some companies, these are decisions "from above" - against internal recommendations. For our UX experts, this means standing their ground and documenting usability problems as usability problems - no matter how great the (political) pressure may be.
- Our experts contact many customers, products, and individual challenges daily. This means they have to be flexible and adapt quickly to new topics. In addition, because of the wide variety of scenarios and user groups, our UX experts need strong methodological skills.

Therefore, from our point of view, UX experts in agencies need additional skills, which we need to look for and develop with our team.

Now that we know how to build the perfect UX team, the question is when to start using UX in product development. And when to stop? That is what we will discuss in the next chapter.

10

When to start and when to stop UX in product development

Chapter ten

When to start and when to stop UX in product development

10.1 What to expect from this chapter

This chapter explores the pivotal role of UX in product development, from the very beginning of the design process to the final stages of a product's lifecycle. You will learn why early starting UX work is essential for aligning teams around a shared vision, avoiding costly missteps, and fostering innovation. We will also discuss the consequences of delayed UX involvement, including inefficiencies, missed opportunities, and higher costs.

The chapter further examines UX's critical role post-launch, highlighting how continuous refinement and adaptation keep products relevant and user-focused. Finally, we will explore the lifecycle of UX, addressing when active involvement in a product might taper off while showing how lessons from past projects can strengthen the next generation of designs.

10.2 When to start UX in product development?

If there is one lesson that resonates universally among our UX Titans, it is this: start UX as early as possible. But why? Let's explore.

10.2.1 Why early UX matters

The earlier UX is involved, the better the chances of building a product that truly resonates with users. Bill Albert uses a vivid analogy: "Imagine if a publisher told an author, 'We love your book idea. Go ahead and write the whole thing, and we'll review it once it's fully done.' It would be disastrous." He continues: "If you do not know the requirements from the start, the chances of failing are enormous."

Uwe Betzin agrees with that. His early-stage work often involves building what Uwe calls the "knowledge framework." He says, "Three-quarters of my time tackling a UX challenge is spent building my knowledge framework. Without this foundational understanding as early as possible, the last quarter – where the solutions emerge – won't happen". Starting early allows UX professionals to gather the necessary knowledge and build the best product.

Additionally, Marc Hassenzahl emphasizes that UX work begins before technical discussions, asking: "Who is this for? Is it for a 70-year-old neighbor or a teenager?" This approach prevents teams from pursuing solutions that may look impressive but fail to address real user challenges. Other Titans agree on that. Gabriela Gomes highlights, "The earlier we can advocate for our users, the greater the impact." Katja Busch adds: "Without early UX, teams risk creating solutions for non-existent problems, leading to costly failures."

Beyond avoiding mistakes, starting UX early fosters alignment among the team and stakeholders. Dominique Winter underlines: "The product vision defines the experience we want to create and becomes a shared mental model for everyone involved." This alignment reduces conflicts and accelerates decision-making throughout the product lifecycle.

Early UX also empowers teams to be more innovative. Teams can confidently explore creative possibilities by focusing on user needs before diving into technical solutions. Thomas Vöhringer-Kuhnt describes: "Starting with a real user problem allows you to open the observation space, exploring diverse possibilities before narrowing down to the best solution." This structured approach ensures that innovation aligns with user goals rather than straying into impractical territory.

We have learned that UX should start as early as possible. But what happens if that is not the case?

10.2.2 The cost of starting late or not starting at all

Delaying UX involvement, or neglecting it entirely, is a gamble that rarely pays off. When UX professionals join a project late, the damage is often already done.

Uwe Betzin illustrates the consequences: "If the UXer joins later, they're panting behind with their understanding. They can't contribute as effectively as needed, and critical decisions affecting the user experience have already been made."

Gabriela Gomes echoes this concern, noting that "retrofitting UX later in the process often means revisiting fundamental decisions, causing delays and inflating costs. " She continues: "Starting late undermines the ability to advocate for the user. Decisions that don't address real needs may already have been made, forcing the team into a reactive stance rather than a proactive one."

Kerstin Dyck paints a grim picture of what happens in these scenarios: "The first product tests may reveal, 'Nobody needs this, nobody wants it.' By then, it's often too late." Without UX at the outset, teams may invest significant resources into creating features or whole products that lack market relevance.

Katja Busch illustrates this risk through the lens of startups: "Many startups fail because they create solutions without real problems. Without market and user insights, investments evaporate into products nobody needs". Whether in startups or established organizations, the absence of early UX results in wasted opportunities and unnecessary expenditure.

Late-stage UX failures can also tarnish a company's reputation. As Thomas Vöhringer-Kuhnt notes, "Without early UX, teams may develop unnecessary or unusable features, resulting in wasted resources and a disconnect with users. In a competitive market, such missteps can have a long-lasting impact on brand perception."

We have seen how starting UX early can lead to innovative, user-centered products and how delaying it can result in costly mistakes and reputational damage. So, if UX starts early and continues throughout the development, does it stop once the product is launched?

10.3 The role of UX post-launch

You have probably already guessed it: The work of UX professionals does not end when a product is launched. Why is that?

10.3.1 Post-launch refinement

The period following a product's release is where UX plays a pivotal role. Katja Busch stresses the importance of this phase, stating, "Post-launch UX is where hypotheses meet reality. This phase offers invaluable opportunities to refine the product and address real-world feedback". During this time, teams can identify gaps, fix unexpected issues, and implement changes to align the product with user needs even better.

Gabriela Gomes highlights the practical challenges of this phase, explaining, "In the starting phase, you need to monitor user feedback and see if there are any bugs or shifting expectations due to external factors." This explains why the UX team needs to continue its work after launch.

10.3.2 Monitoring and adapting

External changes can, of course, not only happen in the starting phase. They can arise all the time. That is why the Titans value maintaining the product's relevance over time. Kerstin Dyck notes: "Even if everything seems perfect now, users' requirements can shift, or broader technological changes might introduce challenges. You have to monitor and adapt – perfection is temporary".

Gabriela Gomes underscores this idea: "Even in maintenance mode, UX work is critical. The world changes, and so do people's expectations. Staying responsive ensures the product remains relevant and valuable." Whether addressing new security requirements, adapting to changing user behaviors, or incorporating technological advancements, UX remains a dynamic and evolving process.

For digital products especially, the need for continual updates is inherent. Marc Hassenzahl describes: "Modern products are interaction streams that require perpetual updates. You can't stop when the world around you changes". This mindset ensures that products remain relevant and user-friendly in a fast-changing world.

Post-launch UX ensures products remain relevant and user-focused through constant refinement and adaptation. But does UX work ever truly stop?

10.4 The lifecycle of UX: When does it end?

In nearly every product's life, there is a point in time when it is discontinued. This could be seen as an ending to active UX activities. Dominique Winter explains: "Active UX involvement stops when a product is strategically discontinued. Until then, every new feature or update shapes the user experience, whether deliberately or not". Similarly, Gert-Dieter Tuzar sees the end of a product's maintenance process as the end of UX: "UX never ends for a product, just like life, it's a spiral. This spiral runs its course unless you're no longer maintaining the product".

Reading this, you might think that UX activities have a defined end. While this is true for one specific product, it is not in general. As Lutz Krauß puts it: "UX work typically concludes when the product is no longer in production or use, though insights from its lifecycle can inform future designs."

Similarly, Kevin Liang adds, "Learning from a past product and processes strengthens the next generation. UX goes on and on and on. Even after a product is no longer actively supported, its lifecycle can offer valuable lessons." This retrospective analysis can help shape the development of new products, ensuring past challenges are not repeated.

So, for many of our UX Titans, the answer is clear: UX rarely, if ever, truly ends.

10.5 Summary

This chapter has explored the crucial role of UX across the entire product lifecycle, starting from its earliest stages to the end of a product's life. The insights from our UX Titans consistently highlight a clear takeaway: UX is not a task limited to any product stage – it is a continuous and strategic process that shapes the success of a product and its successors.

Key Points:

- **Start UX early:** Early UX involvement ensures teams address the correct problems, align stakeholders around a shared vision, and build products that resonate with users. Delaying UX increases the risk of costly mistakes, irrelevant features, and wasted resources.

- **The post-launch phase matters:** Once a product is launched, UX does not stop. Post-launch refinement is critical for validating assumptions, addressing real-world feedback, and adapting to evolving user needs and market conditions.
- **The lifecycle of UX:** Active UX involvement may taper off as a product reaches its end of life, but UX rarely ends entirely. Insights from a product's lifecycle inform future designs, ensuring lessons learned contribute to even stronger, user-centered solutions.

10.6 Our thoughts

Again, the words of our Titans resonate with our own experience. Nevertheless, we would like to add another view from our specific context.

In our day-to-day agency work, we support our clients primarily with products that we call safety, business, or mission-critical. Often, this means making sure the product works right from the start. Think of emergency landing systems in airplanes or heart-lung machines.

There is a strong need for all these products to get usability and UX "right" from the start. If they do not work properly from the start, most likely, someone will die. In addition, there are often regulations in these areas. In the case of medical devices, for example, it has to be proven that use errors do not lead to unacceptable risks before the product is allowed on the market. So, having a usable, safe product is essential here.

Therefore, our daily UX work aims to start as early as possible in the development cycle and bring a safe product with an excellent UX to market. For our products, there is no post-launch phase for refining them. This is because we cannot introduce a product update without much effort, especially in a regulated environment.

So, we do a lot of user testing during development to ensure we know before our clients launch the product that all our assumptions are correct and that it will be successful. We do the same with every product update, although these typically have much longer cycles than products in other areas.

Depending on the area and the products you are working on, the weighting of the individual phases may change. We need a flawless product with an excellent UX before launching, as our customers can only make expensive and time-consuming improvements. In other areas, however, this is not the case. In those areas, user needs can be constantly monitored, and improvements can be integrated into the product quickly without immediately starting with a perfect product. But no matter your specific focus, we fully agree with our Titans that UX goes on and on and on.

Talking about different approaches, products, and industries: Is there one single UX process? Or is it industry, product, or team-specific? That is what we focus on in the next chapter.

11

Is there a single UX process?

Chapter eleven

Is there a single UX process?

11.1 What to expect from this chapter

In this chapter, we address one of the most fundamental questions in UX design: Is there a single process that fits every project or context? Through the perspectives of our UX Titans, we uncover why the answer is no. Afterward, we will discover the core elements that underpin all successful UX processes, including iteration, user understanding, prototyping, and evaluation.

Building on this foundation, we explore how UX processes adapt to meet the demands of specific contexts. The Titans share their insights on:

- **B2B vs. B2C:** Uncover the shared principles and distinct challenges of designing for business and consumer audiences. Learn how stakeholder management, research methods, and design priorities adapt to these differing environments.
- **Industry-Specific Challenges:** Dive into the regulated and high-stakes world of healthcare and aviation, where

safety, compliance, and usability must balance strict regulations and stakeholder complexities.

- **Products vs. Services:** Examine the differences between designing for tangible products and intangible services. Explore how UX processes adapt to suit these contrasting demands, from fixed development cycles to real-time iterative adjustments.

By the end of this chapter, you will have learned from our Titans how the principles of UX provide a consistent foundation while the processes flex to meet the diverse challenges of real-world contexts.

11.2 No, there isn't. Here is why and what every process needs

While browsing the answers from our UX Titans, it quickly becomes clear that everyone agrees that no single UX process can universally apply to every project or context. This might initially seem counterintuitive – are not processes meant to provide structure and consistency? Yet, the Titans argue that this flexibility is one of UX's greatest strengths, allowing designers to adapt to the unique challenges of their environment while remaining anchored to core principles.

Bill Albert captures this sentiment, explaining that many UX processes – Design Thinking, Human-Centered Design, or Lean UX – are variations of the same long-standing principles. "There isn't a single process, but they all follow essentially the same thing, just branded differently," he notes. For Albert and others, the specifics of a process matter less than its ability to ground design decisions in user needs and facilitate iteration.

This iterative nature of UX emerged as a cornerstone across the Titans' discussions. "There must be iterations," emphasizes Kerstin Dyck, "but how often and in what order? That depends." Carmen Fehrenbach echoes this: "The common thread is always iterative work, talking to people, and testing concrete prototypes." For Marc Hassenzahl, iteration drives refinement and invites UXers "to consider the broader implications of their work, from user satisfaction to sustainability and long-term societal impact."

While iteration fuels progress, adaptability ensures fit. Kevin Liang explains, "Adaptability is baked into the UX process. It's not the process but a foundation learners adapt to as they grow." Gabriela Gomes agrees, adding that many processes are designed for ideal conditions – unlimited time and budgets – but in practice, they require adjustment. "In reality, we adapt to constraints, mixing best practices and proven methods.". Therefore, UX processes must flex and respond to organizational culture, time constraints, and resource availability realities.

Asked about UX processes, Uwe Betzin underscores the importance of starting with the right questions. "The key is understanding the problem before rushing into solutions," he explains. He continues: "This is true for the product but also for the process itself." Like other Titans, he advocates having adaptable processes and being adaptable yourself.

Tangible prototyping is another vital element. "The important thing is to talk to real users and create something they can engage with – something concrete," says Carmen Fehrenbach. She argues that "Prototypes transform ideas into something users can interact with, creating opportunities for feedback and collaboration." In her view, prototypes catalyze deeper user understanding and creative exploration.

Finally, the process must remain grounded in continuous evaluation. Gert-Dieter Tuzar highlights: "You need to continuously evaluate whether your solution works from the user's perspective and be prepared to pivot if it doesn't. This also applies to the UX process." Dominique Winter adds, "A successful UX process is empirical and iterative – learning and improving with every cycle."

By weaving these core elements into any UX process, UXers can create flexible and effective workflows.

11.3 Adapting UX processes to specific contexts

To learn how adaptability looks in specific situations, we dive into three key areas where UX processes must flex to meet unique demands: the differences between B2B and B2C, the challenges of regulated and high-stakes industries, and the nuances of designing for products versus services. Through the insights of our Titans, we uncover how foundational principles are tailored to thrive in these diverse environments.

11.3.1 B2B vs. B2C: Shared principles, unique challenges

The overall goal of designing for B2B or B2C is creating user-centered experiences. However, in detail, the challenges they present are vastly different.

In B2B, complexity often dominates the landscape. Decision-making often involves multiple stakeholders, lengthy sales cycles, and a separation between buyers and end users. Bill Albert explains that "B2B is often about more complex, niche applications." The specialized nature of B2B also complicates user research. Kevin Liang highlights this challenge: "In B2B spaces, you often work on very niche, specialized internal software, so your user pools are already quite limited."

In contrast, B2C often emphasizes speed and emotional connection. Consumers can abandon a product anytime, meaning the stakes for first impressions are higher. Matthias Schulz captures this urgency: "Direct customer contact in B2C changes everything. The market reacts instantly – if your product doesn't work, sales plummet." Bill Albert complements: "B2C requires more focus on intuitive interfaces and broad accessibility."

Despite these differences, some aspects remain consistent. Marc Hassenzahl reminds us: "Whether it's B2B or B2C, they are just people. As long as people are involved, they have emotions and experiences." The challenge lies in adapting UX processes to suit the environment while maintaining this shared human-centered foundation.

What often needs to be adapted in UX processes for B2B?

- **Stakeholder management and communication:** In B2B, UX processes often must account for the layered decision-making structure. Throughout the process, UXers must align multiple perspectives – buyers, end users, and stakeholders. Gabriela Gomes notes that "the methods change based on stakeholders and user types."

- **Specialized research approaches:** Given the often smaller and harder-to-reach user pools in B2B, traditional research methods like broad user surveys may not work. Kevin Liang suggests "focusing on niche user interviews and contextual inquiries to gather relevant insights."
- **Integration into workflow and business contexts:** B2B products must seamlessly integrate into existing workflows and organizational systems. Nis Boy Naeve highlights that "business customers are often more tolerant, but the product must still fit well into their workflow, or productivity suffers."

What needs to be adapted in UX processes for B2C?

- **Prioritizing first impressions:** In B2C, the initial interaction often determines whether a user stays or leaves. This requires designing for emotional engagement and ensuring the product is intuitive.
- **Faster iteration cycles:** The immediacy of market feedback in B2C necessitates shorter design and iteration cycles. Matthias Schulz's observation that "the market reacts instantly" makes agility a critical aspect of UX processes in this context.
- **Broad accessibility:** B2C products often cater to a diverse audience, requiring a UX process prioritizing inclusivity and simplicity. This may contrast with B2B, where the user base is often smaller and more specialized.

11.3.2 Industry-specific challenges: Adapting to high stakes

In Chapter 10.6, we have highlighted that designing for regulated and high-stakes industries such as healthcare, aviation, or finance introduces challenges that demand significant adaptation of UX processes. While the fundamental principles of user-centered design remain consistent, these environments impose constraints that require UXers to rethink how they approach research, iteration, and evaluation.

Gabriela Gomes highlights the stakes, explaining: "Mess up UX in entertainment, and someone cancels a subscription. Is it in aviation or healthcare? Lives could be at risk." Similarly, Thomas Vöhringer-Kuhnt points out the unique demands of designing infotainment systems in vehicles: "Operating an infotainment system in a dual-task scenario while driving demands higher standards than designing an app where the user's attention is undivided to one single task."

This heightened responsibility requires UXers to adapt their processes by prioritizing safety, compliance, and long-term usability, often at the expense of speed or creative experimentation.

What often needs to be adapted in UX processes for regulated and high-stakes industries?

- **Longer iteration cycles & stringent research and testing protocols:** In regulated industries, UX processes must include rigorous research and testing stages to ensure that designs meet safety and compliance standards. As

Kerstin Dyck explains, "Products in the medical sector are used for decades, unlike consumer goods, where you can play with trends and shorter cycles." This longevity means usability must be thoroughly validated to ensure reliability over time.

- **Stakeholder collaboration at multiple levels:** UX processes must account for the involvement of various regulatory bodies and high-ranking decision-makers. Kerstin Dyck emphasizes, "The more regulation is involved, the more decision-makers come from outside the company." This requires UXers to communicate their work effectively, often tailoring presentations and prototypes for non-technical audiences outside the company.
- **Balancing usability with compliance:** Dominique Winter underscores that the focus is not always on creating delightful experiences: "Sometimes, it's more about usability than experience." This is the case mainly when the primary goal is to ensure the system functions as intended under strict regulatory frameworks.

11.3.3 Products vs. services: Adapting to tangible and intangible design

When designing products versus services, UX processes must account for fundamental differences in their nature. Products, as tangible entities, often require precision and attention to UX at the interface level. On the other hand, services encompass intangible interactions across multiple touchpoints, requiring broader systems thinking. While both share common principles, their differences demand specific adaptations in how UX processes are planned and executed.

Gabriela Gomes states, "Designing services requires specialized skills to handle abstract processes and complex actor networks." Uwe Betzin adds another key distinction: "With services, it's easier to deliver an MVP and adjust, whereas physical products often require extensive marketing and fixed launches." This means service design can often iterate in real-time, while product design must achieve better stability before release.

What often needs to be adapted in UX processes for products?

- **More usability & UX testing during development:** Products rely heavily on seamless interfaces that users can intuitively navigate, whether physical or digital. Compared to services, changes often are more complicated to facilitate after launch. This results in a higher need for UX testing before release tailored to the product. Thomas Vöhringer-Kuhnt explains that "an infotainment system, for example, demands different evaluation methods than a purely digital service due to its physical constraints and use cases."
- **More fixed development cycles:** Unlike services, products often adhere to fixed launch schedules, requiring UX processes to align with strict marketing and production timelines. This also reduces opportunities for post-launch iteration, making pre-launch validation even more critical. Matthias Schulz adds: "Fixed cycles are even more important for physical products because they cannot be changed after shipping."

What often needs to be adapted in UX processes for services?

- **Broader systems thinking:** Service design requires UXers to think beyond individual touchpoints and consider the entire user journey. Bill Albert emphasizes this need: "Service design demands tools like journey maps and service blueprints to visualize interactions." These tools ensure that every aspect of the service experience –front-stage and behind-the-scenes – is accounted for.
- **Iterative, real-time adjustments:** Services allow greater flexibility post-launch, enabling UXers to refine and iterate based on real-time feedback. Nis Boy Naeve notes, "Discover, design, deliver – this works for both products and services, but the touchpoints for testing and refinement differ. Services are often much more flexible."
- **Experience beyond the interface:** Unlike products, services often extend into physical spaces or human interactions. Marc Hassenzahl explains, "Services like coffee delivery must think beyond the drink itself to the entire experience – like ambiance, interaction, and convenience." This requires UX processes to adapt by integrating environmental and emotional impact into design considerations.

11.4 Summary

UX processes are built on a foundation of universal principles: understanding user needs, iterating on designs, prototyping solutions, and validating through testing. However, as we have seen throughout this chapter, adaptability is the key to ensuring these principles remain effective in UX professionals' diverse contexts.

- **No single UX process:** The Titans agree – there is no one-size-fits-all UX process. Instead, successful UX relies on tailoring workflows to specific challenges while maintaining a flexible, user-centered approach. Iteration and adaptability provide the backbone for meeting real-world constraints and expectations.
- **Adapting for B2B vs. B2C:** While B2B and B2C share a human-centered foundation, UXers must adapt their processes to address unique challenges:
    - In B2B, stakeholder management, niche research methods, and workflow integration often require special focus.
    - In B2C, first impressions, agility in iteration, and broad accessibility are often critical to success.
- **Adapting for industry-specific challenges:** High-stakes and regulated industries demand rigorous adjustments:
    - Longer research and testing cycles ensure compliance and safety.
    - Stakeholder collaboration extends to regulatory bodies and decision-makers from outside the company.
    - Usability may take precedence over delightful experiences when functionality is critical.

- **Adapting for products vs. services:** Designing for tangible products versus intangible services requires distinct shifts:
    - Products demand precise usability & UX testing, more fixed development cycles, and stable pre-launch validation, especially if the product is physical.
    - Services thrive on broader systems thinking, real-time iteration, and a focus on experiences beyond the interface.

11.5 Our thoughts

As mentioned in the previous "Our thoughts" chapters, we work mainly on complex B2B products in an agency context. Often, the products we design are regulated. Therefore, our experience is mainly in this product area and less in the design of services.

Working as an agency means you come into contact with many different UX processes. Therefore, we have an extensive overview and have worked with countless process variations.

From our point of view, the two most important aspects of any UX process are the regular involvement of users at the earliest possible stage, combined with the will of all parties involved to adapt the product to the users. If both were the case, then the process has always been successful. If not, the products always fail in the end.

Therefore, these two points are the fundamentals. All other details may make the process better or faster. However, they are less responsible for the overall success of the process.

We do not mean to suggest that the details can be ignored. In medical devices, for example, everything must be documented. Failure to document can be catastrophic, as approval may be denied. So, these "details" can have significant consequences. What we want to say, however, is that if you focus only on the details and ignore the two fundamentals (involve users as early as possible and adapt the product accordingly) mentioned above, then the product will initially fail.

With that said, we leave the process world and jump to the next important question: How does the budget affect UX efforts?

12

How does your budget influence the way you approach UX?

Chapter twelve

How does your budget influence the way you approach UX?

12.1 What to expect from this chapter

Navigating the world of UX means often adapting to diverse challenges, and one of the most pressing is working within budget constraints. Whether faced with a tight €1,000 budget or a generous €100,000, the question remains: How do you deliver meaningful, user-centered results within your financial limits?

In this chapter, we explore how varying budgets influence UX strategies. You will discover how to prioritize, innovate, and maximize the value of your resources. This chapter will equip you with approachable ideas for any budget scenario, from guerrilla tactics and quick wins to building sustainable UX frameworks.

12.2 Making every euro count: UX on a budget

Have you ever wondered what our Titans would do with different budgets? Well, we did. And we asked them. Here is what they answered:

12.2.1 How would you do UX if you had a budget of 1.000€?

For many UX Titans, 1.000€ is an exceptionally tight budget – barely enough to make a significant impact. Yet, their responses highlight innovative approaches to extract value even within constraints, focusing on prioritization, creativity, and stakeholder engagement.

While some responses highlight the challenge with a touch of humor, they underscore the limitations of such a small budget. Lutz Krauß jokes: "With that amount, I'd take my neighbor out for dinner and casually ask for feedback on my product." Other Titans also made similar jokes.

Although eating is always a good idea in the authors' opinion, we would like to elaborate on other approaches, too. Uwe Betzin suggests assembling key stakeholders for a focused workshop: "Bring product specialists together for a day. Identify the users' trickiest problems, sketch key screens on a whiteboard, and define what needs to be prioritized." Dominique Winter echoes this approach: "I'd organize a two-hour session with the core team to establish a shared vision and align everyone around a common goal."

For some Titans, such a budget represents an opportunity to increase organizational awareness of UX. Katja Busch describes her method: "I'd conduct guerrilla interviews to surface critical business risks. Then, I'd present these insights to stakeholders to advocate for a larger budget." Kevin Liang emphasizes the connection between limited budgets and UX maturity: "Low budgets often reflect low UX maturity. I'd focus on educating stakeholders about why UX matters and advocating for its role in the development process."

Despite the constraints, engaging directly with end users remains a priority for many Titans. Bill Albert proposes a simple but effective tactic: "I'd buy coffee gift cards, find users, and gather quick feedback. Then I'd iterate and repeat – insights don't have to be expensive." Gabriela Gomes shares the importance of customer understanding: "I'd use the money to conduct user interviews and uncover needs. Without understanding users, nothing else matters."

Others also outline lean, hands-on methods to generate actionable insights quickly. Gert-Dieter Tuzar describes a compact UX sprint: "One expert, two days: observe users, identify pain points, sketch concepts, and evaluate them with five users. It's a small-scale process but delivers clear direction for development." Matthias Schulz adds: "A skilled UX designer could conduct a few interviews, create rough prototypes, and test a first iteration. It's all about maximizing impact within minimal resources."

Even with such a limited budget, the consensus among the Titans is clear: it can still drive meaningful results through workshops, guerrilla tactics, or user feedback. The key lies in careful prioritization and leveraging small-scale activities to lay the groundwork for more. Talking about more: What would our Titans do with 10.000€?

12.2.2 How would you do UX if you had a budget of 10.000€?

With 10.000€, UX efforts allow more structured approaches to engage users and iterate on designs. For many UX Titans, this budget represents a turning point where the focus shifts toward more intensive usability testing, prototyping, and gaining deeper user insights.

For Ulf Schubert, usability testing takes center stage: "If this is your first 10.000€, invest in testing. Watching users interact with your product can reveal the most significant issues. The insights you gain here outweigh everything else in impact."

Gabriela Gomes echoes this sentiment, emphasizing a lean prototyping approach: "Quick prototypes tested against your main assumptions help eliminate big problems early. With this clarity, you can secure more funding or refine the vision."

Gert-Dieter Tuzar also recommends using the budget for iterative user testing: "Interactive prototypes reveal subtleties that static designs can't. By cycling through multiple tests, you can refine the user flow and the design experience."

Others focus on combining qualitative and quantitative methods to gain well-rounded insights. Bill Albert explains: "A deeper dive into interviews and surveys provides a robust understanding of user needs. If the context is critical, field research rounds out the approach beautifully."

Dominique Winter takes a team-focused approach, using the budget to build sustainable structures: "I'd use the 10.000€ to empower the team, kickoff workshops, iterative meetings, and reflective sessions. It's about creating structures that last, ensuring the budget isn't just a quick fix but a foundation for long-term success."

Marc Hassenzahl suggests scaling up incrementally: "You can stretch a 10.000€ budget with smaller workshops, squeezed-in interviews, and incremental evaluations. While it won't solve everything, this iterative approach ensures you move forward systematically."

Even with a mid-sized budget, prioritization remains crucial. The Titans agree that 10.000€ can deliver meaningful results when used strategically to focus on high-impact activities like usability testing, iterative prototyping, and fostering team alignment. By building on these approaches, organizations can create user-centered designs while laying the groundwork for future growth.

12.2.3 How would you do UX if you had a budget of 100.000€?

With 100.000€, UX work reaches a new level of potential, enabling a mix of ambitious research, iterative design, and team development. For many UX Titans, this budget marks the transition from short-term tactics to strategic, long-term investments in user experience.

Uwe Betzin highlights the transformative power of embedding a UX expert: "Continuous staffing transforms the UX function.

Rather than being called in reactively, the expert becomes an integral part of the team, guiding the UX maturity of the entire project." Similarly, Tobias Oberpaul suggests a strategic allocation to support multiple products or specialists: "If your company manages multiple products, having dedicated UX experts for each can deepen their understanding of the individual domains. Alternatively, pairing a UX researcher with a designer ensures thorough user insights inform every design decision." He also emphasizes the value of documentation: "Good documentation prevents the iterative learning cycle from being disrupted. Otherwise, teams risk reinventing the wheel repeatedly."

Marc Hassenzahl proposes investing in visionary prototypes: "Prototyping isn't just about building products; it's about sparking ideas, learning, and uncovering better directions. High-fidelity prototypes or detailed scenarios can generate excitement internally and externally." Gert-Dieter Tuzar would also invest in a better prototype: "With this budget, you can move from a Minimum Viable Product to a Minimum Lovable Product – a prototype polished enough to excite users and stakeholders while ensuring clarity and engagement."

Advanced research methodologies become viable with this budget. Gert-Dieter Tuzar advocates for immersive and high-quality data collection: "We often avoid field research due to its expense, but it yields unmatched insights. At 100.000€, you can expand your methodological toolkit from eye-tracking studies to VR-driven immersion tests." Similarly, Bill Albert stresses the importance of a bigger toolkit: "With 100.000€, I'd look at how this product stacks up against the competition, gathering qualitative and quantitative insights."

Kerstin Dyck recommends focusing on a high-visibility initiative to create a ripple effect: "A smaller, high-visibility project allows teams to demonstrate success and build momentum. It's about choosing an impactful starting point that resonates across the organization." Gabriela Gomes adds: "It's about making a case for the next 100.000€ – establishing the foundation or scaling up an existing practice to demonstrate long-term value."

For others, the budget offers an opportunity to raise UX maturity to another level. Dominique Winter highlights team enablement: "With 100.000€, I'd invest in empowering the team through workshops, coaching, and additional resources. It's about building internal capabilities for sustained impact."

The Titans agree that 100.000€ is a transformative budget capable of advancing UX maturity, improving research quality, and fostering collaboration across teams. By using it strategically, organizations can achieve impactful results and build a strong case for continued investment in user experience.

12.3 Summary

The insights from our UX Titans reveal that while budget constraints shape the scope of UX efforts, creativity, and strategic prioritization enable meaningful outcomes at any financial level. From €1,000 to 100.000€, the key lies in adapting approaches to maximize impact while maintaining user focus.

At 1.000€, the consensus among our Titans is that while the budget is highly restrictive, it can still spark valuable insights. Guerrilla tactics, workshops, and quick user interviews are the preferred methods to generate momentum, raise UX awareness, and identify critical issues that lay the foundation for future investment.

With 10.000€, UX work becomes more structured, allowing for more intensive usability testing, iterative prototyping, and deeper user engagement. This budget enables teams to tackle more complex challenges, build inclusivity, and refine designs through multiple iterations while focusing on user needs and aligning with business goals.

At 100.000€, UX efforts reach a transformative level, where organizations can integrate UX as a strategic function. Whether through embedding full-time UX professionals, investing in high-quality research, or creating visionary prototypes, this budget supports a balance of short-term wins and long-term impact. The focus shifts toward scaling UX maturity, building internal capacity, and fostering a user-centric culture.

Across all scenarios, the Titans emphasize the importance of prioritization, collaboration, and continuous learning. Regardless of the budget size, successful UX efforts are driven by a commitment to understanding users, iterating on insights, and aligning designs with user needs and organizational goals.

12.4 Our thoughts

While working in our agency and beforehand at Technische Universität Darmstadt, one thing has become clear: you can create effective UX on any budget. From our point of view, good UX work is less a question of budget and more a question of approach and environment.

Small startups and students working on student projects can get user feedback with little or no budget (at least for easy-to-find user groups). Of course, you can also generate user feedback by hiring a proven professional or even a specialized agency to conduct a methodologically sound, large-scale study. In this case, the budget needs will naturally increase.

Either way, you get user feedback at a completely different price point. The question of which approach is better and which budget you should spend depends on what you want to achieve. While one approach requires spending much of your own time learning from experts, finding users, and conducting and analyzing interviews, the second approach allows you to buy a ready-made professional result. Both methods lead to the goal of gathering user feedback. The difference is how quickly, effectively, conveniently, and with what quality you get there and how much of your own time you have to invest.

Speaking of quality: From the feedback of our Titans, we saw that experts can produce high-quality results for almost any budget. We have already mentioned this before, but we cannot stress this enough: This is not the case when methodological knowledge (e.g., survey techniques) is lacking. Then, even the most enormous budget will not help because you cannot spend it wisely. As a UX professional, the limiting factor is often not the budget but time. As a non-expert, the limiting factor is quality. To achieve a sufficiently high level of quality, you need time (which you use to become an expert yourself) or budget (to pay experts to achieve the quality).

We want to add another thought: students without a budget and experts with a huge budget can find the wrong answers if they do not know the right questions. Therefore, in addition to the path choice, a second point is important to us: the desired goal.

One of the best investments you can make in UX is to be clear about what you want to achieve and then manage your activities to get there. When managing activities, it is often helpful to identify the most crucial problem and focus on solving that (and only that).

What the most crucial problem is depends on your point of view. For example, it could be testing the assumptions that must be true for the product to deliver customer value. It could also be a detail deep in the most important workflow that causes active customers to look for alternatives. It could also be a team member who is supposed to "do" UX but needs more training.

We advise investing time in identifying the goal and the most pressing problem. Then, determine how you want to solve the problem. That way, any budget will be put to the best use, no matter how large.

In this chapter, we discussed budgets and the path to reach the desired goal. In the next chapter, we will look at another topic influencing the path: UX trends.

13

Navigating the trends transforming UX design

Chapter thirteen

Navigating the trends transforming UX design

13.1 What to expect from this chapter

In this chapter, you will gain insights into the key trends shaping the future of UX, as identified in our Titans' interviews between 2023 and 2024. From technological advancements like AI and AR/VR to shifts in organizational strategy and user expectations, we explore how these forces are transforming the discipline.

You will discover how emerging technologies redefine interaction paradigms, creating more intuitive, immersive, and personalized experiences. At the same time, trends such as sustainability, accessibility, and simplification are challenging UXers to design with greater responsibility and inclusivity.

13.2 Why trends matter in UX

The world of UX is ever-changing, influenced by rapid technological advancements, evolving user expectations, and broader societal challenges. Understanding trends is essential for creating relevant, impactful, and future-proof designs. Here is why our Titans see importance in trends:

- **Anticipating change & adapting to it:** Trends provide a window into the future, helping UXers prepare for shifts in their tools, processes, and users' needs. As Ulf Schubert explains: "What we're doing today may seem efficient, but tomorrow it could be too slow for what's needed."
- **Driving strategic impact with innovation:** Trends allow UXers to demonstrate their value beyond the confines of individual projects. They show how UX can drive innovation and align with organizational goals. Nis Boy Naeve reflects: "Recognizing what's ahead allows us to position design as a strategic driver, not just an implementation function."
- **A broader responsibility:** Trends often carry ethical and societal implications, requiring UXers to think critically about their role. Understanding these shifts is more than keeping up; it is about designing responsibly. Marc Hassenzahl captures this sentiment: "We need to question our decisions and understand their impact – on people, society, and the future."

By engaging with trends, UX professionals can anticipate change, adapt to new challenges, and contribute to shaping the discipline's future. Let us now look deeper at the trends our Titans see, including their possibilities and possible challenges.

13.3 The transformative role of AI in UX

According to our Titans, Artificial Intelligence (AI) is one of the most significant forces shaping the future of UX. From automating repetitive tasks to enabling new forms of interaction, AI offers immense opportunities to enhance the design process and create more intuitive, impactful experiences. However, it also brings challenges – particularly around ethics, transparency, and inclusivity – that UXers must navigate carefully.

13.3.1 Using AI as a tool for UX work

AI is revolutionizing how UXers approach their work. Gabriela Gomes highlights this transformation: "AI allows us to offload repetitive tasks, enabling UXers to focus on strategy and impact earlier in the process."

This shift is especially evident in research and prototyping. Ulf Schubert envisions a future: "Machines summarize feedback, allowing UXers to ask smarter questions and move faster."

Generative AI also offers tools to streamline design creation. Kerstin Dyck explains: "AI will draft interfaces based on design systems and user requirements, democratizing UX while allowing UX experts to focus on other tasks."

However, this automation comes with risks. Katja Busch cautions: "AI can produce polished but misleading results, tempting people to accept outputs without questioning their quality." In her opinion, UXers must remain critical and discerning, ensuring AI outputs are validated and refined for real-world use. She remarks, "This problem is even more challenging if misleading results match stakeholders' expectations." Therefore, according to her, UXers must be able to explain to stakeholders what they see from a user perspective without stepping on their toes.

13.3.2 Using AI as a new UI possibility

AI-powered conversational interfaces, such as chatbots and virtual assistants, reshape how users interact with technology. Dominique Winter describes this evolution: "Conversational UIs will create relationship-level interactions between users and systems." Nis Boy Naeve agrees: "Conversational AI will fundamentally change interaction patterns." This is seen as a huge possibility for UX since these tools may enable more natural, human-like interactions, creating opportunities to build stronger connections.

However, as Marc Hassenzahl puts it: "The social dynamics of AI-driven interactions pose UX design challenges." A lot of our Titans agreed on those ethical challenges. Therefore, we have dedicated the following section to this topic, even though it is not directly considered a trend but a companion.

13.3.3 Ethical implications of AI in UX

As AI becomes increasingly integrated into UX, ethical considerations grow more critical. Sarah Diefenbach highlights this need: "How do I know I'm dealing with AI? How trustworthy are its decisions?" Marc Hassenzahl adds: "Users must understand whether they interact with a human or a machine."

Another major concern is biases in AI systems. Kerstin Dyck reflects: "We must prevent AI algorithms from reflecting the biases of those who program them."

Furthermore, UXers must carefully evaluate whether AI is always the right solution. Marc Hassenzahl reminds us: "Just because we can do something with AI doesn't mean we should. We need to question our decisions and their broader implications."

13.4 Redefining interaction paradigms

We already talked about AI-driven user interfaces. Besides that, other technologies change the interactions between humans and technologies. This section will focus on emerging technologies that blend physical and digital worlds, create immersive experiences, and enable more natural connections between humans and systems.

13.4.1 Augmented and virtual realities (AR/VR)

AR and VR technologies are poised to revolutionize UX across industries. Tobias Oberpaul explains: "AR and VR are at the start of their potential; transformative applications lie ahead." Matthias Schulz also sees potential in using AR/VR: "AR/VR will grow in education and beyond. It's extremely interesting for teachers and learning environments." Thomas Vöhringer-Kuhnt highlights: "AR enriches interfaces, for example, in automotive head-up displays, center information displays and digital rearview mirrors that integrate additional information or guidance for drivers directly related to the real-world environment."

Despite their potential, AR and VR still face barriers to widespread adoption, including cost, accessibility, and the need for thoughtful integration into real-world applications. These challenges underscore the importance of exploring AR/VR as functional and emotional user engagement tools.

13.4.2 The Metaverse: Expanding digital ecosystems

The metaverse offers a new paradigm for human-technology interaction, creating interconnected digital environments where users can engage in virtual worlds. Sarah Diefenbach shares her mixed feelings: "Parallel worlds already exist, but their influence on daily life remains uncertain. However, they are undeniably shaping niche applications and communities."

The metaverse pushes UXers to rethink traditional interaction models, emphasizing seamless, immersive experiences. However, it also requires a balance between innovation and accessibility to ensure these environments are inclusive and meaningful for diverse users.

13.4.3 Multimodal experiences

Multimodal interaction is emerging as a key trend. Gabriela Gomes explains: "Multimodal experiences, combining physical and digital interactions, will enhance accessibility and expand how users engage with technology. We have so many devices in our homes, and this idea that everything is connected has been around for a long time, but now it's exciting to see how it plays with AI and a serious commitment to accessibility and inclusive design."

These experiences often involve interconnected devices. Lutz Krauß offers an example: "Imagine wooden toys equipped with NFC that trigger digital actions – these interactions open up playful, tangible possibilities."

Multimodal experiences can transform industries like healthcare and automotive by offering more intuitive and inclusive interfaces. Still, they also require careful attention to ensure a high UX and value across diverse contexts.

13.5 Personalization and accessibility: Designing for individuals and inclusion

As UX evolves, our Titans see two interconnected trends shape how we approach design: personalization and accessibility. Together, they reflect the growing demand for tailored and inclusive user experiences.

13.5.1 Data-driven personalization

Advances in data analytics and computational power are enabling experiences to be customized to individual users in real-time. Thomas Vöhringer-Kuhnt highlights this trend: "Personalization will play a big role, leveraging real-time data for tailored user interfaces. By outsourcing computation to the cloud, systems can now use data practically in real-time to offer meaningful customization."

This capability allows products to deliver uniquely tailored experiences through personalized interfaces, adaptive recommendations, or predictive interactions. However, this raises critical questions about privacy, transparency, and user control over their data that UXers must consider.

13.5.2 Inclusive design and accessibility regulations

Accessibility ensures that products are usable by everyone, regardless of their abilities or circumstances. It has long been a cornerstone of good UX, but new regulations like the European Accessibility Act drive a renewed emphasis on inclusivity. Gabriela Gomes describes this as a transformative moment: "The time has finally come when companies confront the cycle of exclusion they've been part of. Embracing accessibility drives innovation and broadens the scope of products for everyone."

In addition, the importance of assistive technologies is growing. Sarah Diefenbach explains: "Technologies that act as interaction partners or supporters will play an even bigger role in the future."

13.5.3 The interplay between personalization and accessibility

Personalization and accessibility are often seen as separate concerns, but our Titans argue they complement each other in practice. Oliver Kulpi highlights: "Personalization can make interfaces more accessible by tailoring them to individual preferences and needs, while accessibility ensures that personalized systems work for all users, including those with disabilities." For example, a personalized interface could adapt font sizes or color schemes for visually impaired users, creating a more inclusive experience.

However, this interplay requires careful balance. While personalization relies heavily on user data, accessibility mandates that systems be universally usable, even without extensive data collection. UXers must navigate these tensions to create inclusive and adaptive experiences.

13.6 Green UX, sustainability, and planet-centric design

According to our Titans, sustainability is becoming a central trend in UX as users and companies increasingly prioritize environmentally conscious practices. This shift challenges UXers to rethink how they design systems, considering the immediate user impact and the broader environmental and societal implications.

Green UX focuses on minimizing resource use and designing with sustainability at the forefront. By adopting green UX principles, UXers can create experiences that minimize waste and extend the lifecycle of products and services. Nis Boy Naeve underscores the urgency of these changes: "Climate change will influence resource-conscious product and UX design, pushing us to rethink how we create and consume."

Kerstin Dyck emphasizes how user expectations drive this transformation: "More users incorporate sustainability into their purchasing decisions, and companies are embedding it into their values."

Marc Hassenzahl adds that designing for sustainability often goes beyond traditional UX considerations: "Sustainability requires us to think about how our design processes and outcomes affect not just users, but the society." He continues: "If you go even further and put society in a more general context, planet-centric design becomes a thing. It challenges us to consider the broader implications of our products for the planet."

By integrating planet-centric principles, UXers can align their work with global sustainability goals, ensuring their designs contribute to a better future for both people and the planet.

13.7 Simplification and deceleration

Many users seek simplicity and slower, more thoughtful interactions as the digital world accelerates. This countertrend – focused on decluttering experiences and reducing complexity – addresses the growing need for intuitive and calming technologies rather than overwhelming ones.

Lutz Krauß reflects this trend: "Slow experiences like slow food and slow work reflect the need for less cluttered interfaces." Gert-Dieter Tuzar adds: "Reducing interface complexity will streamline human-machine interactions, creating intuitive and efficient environments."

According to our Titans, simplification does improve UX in many and fosters a sense of control and ease. By stripping away excess and focusing on what truly matters to users, UXers can craft elegant and functional experiences. This movement challenges the industry to prioritize thoughtful design over feature-heavy solutions, ensuring every interaction feels purposeful and straightforward.

13.8 Bridging disciplines and new roles in UX

As the boundaries between disciplines blur, UX becomes more collaborative and holistic. Bill Albert highlights: "UX, CX, and service design are the same thing at the core. They're about trying to deliver a great experience, especially the growth of service design. Their convergence will redefine how we think about user journeys."

This shift calls for a broader perspective that transcends traditional UX. UXers are increasingly required to think systemically, considering the entire ecosystem of user interactions across physical and digital touchpoints. Such a mindset enhances user satisfaction and ensures that products and services align with larger business goals.

To support this evolution, new roles are emerging that bridge the gaps between design, engineering, and business.

13.9 Increased focus on UX in management

As UX becomes a critical driver of business strategy, there is a noticeable shift toward UX management and enterprise UX. Organizations recognize the value of embedding UX strategically, ensuring it aligns with overarching business goals and drives long-term success.

Ulf Schubert emphasizes the strategic importance of UX in management:

"I believe this whole experience mindset belongs at the management level, regardless of whether it's UX, CX, or EX. And I can see that it is getting there." Similarly, Uwe Betzin adds: "UX in management is still an untapped field, but it holds significant potential for influencing organizational strategy."

As UX becomes more integrated into organizational structures, strategic UX leaders are needed to guide teams, foster cross-functional collaboration, and advocate for the user at the executive level. This trend is reshaping how UX is perceived – not just as a functional capability but as a cornerstone of business innovation and success.

13.10 Summary

This chapter has explored the transformative trends shaping the future of UX, as shared by our Titans. These trends highlight the evolving demands of technology, society, and business on the discipline, challenging UXers to adapt and innovate.

- **Why trends matter:** Understanding trends helps UXers anticipate changes, drive innovation, and design responsibly, balancing their impact on users, society, and the environment.
- **The transformative role of AI:** AI is revolutionizing UX work by automating tasks, creating conversational interfaces, and pushing ethical boundaries. While AI offers significant

opportunities, it demands critical evaluation and a focus on fairness and transparency.

- **Redefining interaction paradigms:** Technologies like AR/VR, the metaverse, and multimodal interactions reshape how users engage with technology. These advances blend physical and digital worlds, creating immersive and intuitive experiences requiring thoughtful integration.
- **Personalization and accessibility:** These interconnected trends reflect a growing demand for tailored and inclusive experiences. Together, they ensure that systems are adaptable to individual needs while remaining accessible to all users.
- **Green UX, sustainability, and planet-centric design:** UX embraces sustainability and moves toward green practices and planet-centric approaches that align design decisions with broader environmental goals.
- **Simplification and deceleration:** In a fast-paced digital landscape, users value simplicity and intuitive interactions, emphasizing the importance of streamlined interfaces and thoughtful design.
- **Bridging disciplines and new roles:** UX is increasingly collaborative, merging with CX and service design while fostering new roles to bridge gaps between teams and disciplines.
- **Increased focus on UX in management:** As UX becomes integral to business strategy, there is a growing need for strategic leaders to align UX with organizational goals and drive its influence at the executive level.

13.11 Our thoughts

Reflecting on the trends shared by our Titans, it becomes clear that our Titans have a dual role. On one hand, they are shaping today's user experiences. On the other hand, they are working on the methodical and strategic levels of the UX field itself.

The same is true for trends themselves. Our Titans found trends that will shape the way users interact with technology. One example they came up with is AI, which reshapes how users interact with computers. Other trends focus on the UX field and how UXers will work. An example stated in this area is how UX will be interwoven with management.

As with any collection of trends, the test will be time. It will be fascinating to see which trends gain momentum and reshape the UX landscape and which fade into the background.

Since there was some time from the interviews done in 2023 and 2024 to writing and publishing the book, we can already tell that AI heavily influences UX. Even to the point that some experts state there will be a "UX reset" reshaping the entire UX industry[38].

Regardless of which trends emerge as dominant, the ongoing evolution of technology and the UX field will undoubtedly lead to exciting opportunities and challenges for UXers to explore.

Building on what we have learned in this chapter, we asked the Titans which fields of UX will be most relevant in the future. Let us find out what they answered.

[38] In "The UX Reckoning: Prepare for 2025 and Beyond" (Nielsen Norman Group, January 10, 2025), the authors highlight the challenges facing UX professionals in 2025, including a tough job market and declining organizational UX maturity, while emphasizing AI's transformative role in enhancing design tools and shifting UX toward outcome-oriented, user-focused practices. The article urges UXers to adapt by leveraging AI, returning to core principles, and developing deeper skills to navigate an evolving field. https://www.nngroup.com/articles/ux-reset-2025/

14

What are the fields where UX will be most relevant in the future?

Chapter fourteen

What are the fields where UX will be most relevant in the future?

14.1 What to expect from this chapter

In this chapter, we explore the key fields where our Titans believe UX will have the greatest impact in the future. Building on the trends discussed in Chapter 13, such as ethical AI, simplification, and sustainability, we shift the focus from overarching movements to specific industries and areas where UX professionals can make transformative contributions.

This chapter examines five critical fields – healthcare, sustainability, artificial intelligence, the public sector, and universal applications – showcasing how UX can address pressing global challenges. Whether improving patient outcomes, enabling eco-conscious decisions, or crafting seamless civic services, UX's ability to create human-centered solutions stands at the forefront of innovation.

14.2 Fields where UX will drive change

Building on the trends explored in Chapter 13, such as AI, simplification, and sustainability, this chapter focuses on specific fields where our Titans see UX driving transformative change. These fields illustrate how UX professionals can address pressing global challenges, creating human-centered solutions that align with societal values and needs.

14.2.1 Healthcare: Transforming Patient Experiences and Medical Solutions

Healthcare is one of the fields where our Titans foresee UX making significant advancements in the coming years. The demand for user-centered design in this sector is growing as outdated systems and processes give way to patient-first approaches, better-designed medical products, and more accessible health technologies.

Bill Albert emphasizes the increasing attention healthcare UX is receiving: "I only see UX increasing in healthcare [...] looking at the patient experience that's been around for a little while, but I think that's only going to get more and more attention because it's got such a strong potential upside."

Similarly, Carmen Fehrenbach describes, "The entire hospital and medical operation feels like something from the 1980s. Patients have to adapt to the system rather than the system adapting to them. This needs to change." She sees UX as a way to drive a values-based transformation in healthcare, shifting the focus toward systems that offer more human-centered experiences.

The medical technology industry is also poised for a UX revolution, where better design translates directly into business success. Matthias Schulz highlights this connection: "In the medical technology market, UX will grow even more. I hope it's not just because of legal requirements but because people realize better UX leads to better sales and product success."

In this evolving landscape, UX has the potential to address inefficiencies, improve outcomes, and humanize healthcare systems. According to our Titans, the healthcare sector's adaptation to technological advancements and societal expectations presents a vast opportunity for UX professionals. By focusing on creating solutions that are not just functional but empathetic and impactful, UX can reshape how patients and practitioners engage with healthcare services.

14.2.2 Sustainability: designing for environmental responsibility

As we saw in Chapter 13.6, sustainability is a field where UX has the power to drive meaningful behavioral and systemic changes. We have already learned from our Titans that they expect to see more "Green UX" and planet-centric designs in the future.

Bill Albert takes this even further: "UX can guide users to make better decisions, whether choosing a reusable product over a disposable one or understanding the carbon impact of their choices." By simplifying complex data and presenting it intuitively, UX can empower users to make informed decisions that align with their values.

Carmen Fehrenbach echoes this need for transparency: "People want to make sustainable choices but often don't have the information they need. UX can make this information clear [...] like having a fairness score that tells you how ethically a product was produced." By integrating transparency into interfaces, designers can ensure users understand the environmental and social impact of their consumption habits.

Beyond digital interfaces, UX can influence perceptions through physical and tactile experiences. Guido Meier-Arendt explains: "If a surface feels like bamboo fibers or natural materials, this tactile connection reinforces the perception of sustainability. UX influences both the physical and digital aspects of user perception." This demonstrates how UX can extend its impact on sensory experiences, enhancing users' emotional connections to eco-friendly choices and using materials to showcase sustainable design.

14.2.3 Artificial intelligence: Ensuring ethical and usable systems

As discussed in Chapter 13.3, trends like conversational interfaces and ethical AI are reshaping how users interact with technology. Our Titans believe UX professionals are uniquely positioned to guide these advancements and address the challenges they bring.

Kerstin Dyck underscores the potential risks if UX is not involved: "AI systems can easily go wrong if we don't ensure they align with societal and user values. UX has a critical role in preventing harm and ensuring ethical design." With AI's increasing integration into everyday life, UX can safeguard against creating systems that alienate or confuse users.

Building on this, Guido Meier-Arendt highlights the potential: "Future AI-driven interactions will involve natural, intuitive interfaces, like conversational systems or virtual environments. UX must ensure these experiences are seamless." Whether designing voice-activated assistants or immersive virtual spaces, UX practitioners must ensure these systems feel intuitive and human-centric. Nis Boy Naeve adds that this might come with a role change for UXers: "If UX professionals understand how to define their role properly in AI design, they can make these systems trustworthy, intuitive, and even fun."

14.2.4 Public sector: Innovating civic services for everyone

The public sector is another field where our Titans see UX drive transformative change. As governments worldwide address challenges such as climate change, socio-economic inequality, and public health crises, UX professionals can be critical in ensuring that civic systems are inclusive, efficient, and accessible to all.

Kevin Liang envisions: "I hope UX will be more prominent in civic spaces, maybe in government. [...] What they do is for the people. I hope to see more of that." His perspective highlights how UX can shift focus from government-process-driven systems to people-centered solutions, ensuring that public services meet diverse populations' needs.

The COVID-19 pandemic underscored the urgency of improving public systems. Gabriela Gomes reflects on this lesson: "The pandemic showed us how critical it is to have digital systems that work for everyone, not just the tech-savvy." Better-designed public systems can ensure equitable access to resources, from healthcare portals to social services, reducing barriers that often exclude vulnerable groups.

14.2.5 Beyond industry boundaries: UX as a universal force

UX is increasingly recognized as a universal force that extends beyond specific industries, shaping how humans interact with technology in nearly every context. From consumer-facing applications to behind-the-scenes industrial processes, our Titans emphasize that wherever humans and technology intersect, UX has a vital role to play.

Marc Hassenzahl succinctly captures this perspective: "There's no field of human activity untouched by technology. UX is everywhere, shaping interactions between humans and systems." His words highlight the pervasive nature of UX and its ability to influence how people experience even the most unexpected domains.

Kevin Liang provides an example of UX breaking into traditionally non-digital fields: "Even industries like tire manufacturing, which you wouldn't associate with UX, are starting to realize its value. UX is becoming a growing field across many domains." This shift reflects the growing recognition that good design and UX are essential, even in fields not typically associated with user experience.

Gert-Dieter Tuzar reinforces this idea by focusing on the universality of UX across services and products: "In every field where humans are involved – whether it's products or services – UX plays a central role." From streamlining internal business systems to enhancing consumer experiences, UX professionals increasingly create human-centered solutions across diverse applications.

According to our Titans, this universality is driven by rising expectations for usability and UX. As users interact with well-designed systems in one part of their lives, they expect similar quality and intuitiveness across all their interactions, whether in consumer products, industrial tools, or public services. By embracing this expanded role, UX professionals can influence individual industries and the broader human experience.

14.3 Summary

This chapter explored five critical fields where UX has the potential to drive transformative change, as identified by our Titans. By shifting the focus from trends to specific industries and areas, we demonstrated how UX professionals are uniquely positioned to solve pressing challenges and create human-centered solutions that align with societal values.

- In **healthcare**, UX can revolutionize patient experiences, streamline medical systems, and shift toward empathetic, patient-first approaches that enable healthcare professionals to focus on the patients instead of the systems.
- In **sustainability**, UX is vital in guiding eco-conscious behaviors, promoting transparency, and simplifying complex systems to make sustainable decisions accessible and actionable.

- **Artificial intelligence** offers challenges and opportunities, with UX ensuring ethical, intuitive, and human-centric designs in a rapidly evolving technological landscape.
- In the **public sector**, UX professionals have the chance to improve civic systems, making them inclusive, efficient, and empowering for all citizens.
- The universality of UX shines through **in fields beyond traditional industry boundaries**, where it influences interactions across consumer products, industrial tools, and non-digital spaces.

14.4 Our thoughts

One observation stands out as we reflect on the fields outlined in this chapter: many are deeply interconnected. Meta-topics like artificial intelligence, sustainability, and accessibility increasingly shape healthcare systems and public sector applications. For example, AI might power a healthcare application while the same system integrates accessibility to serve diverse patient populations and sustainability to meet environmental goals.

This interconnectedness highlights the strategic role of UX as an enabler across all fields. UX professionals are not merely solving isolated problems but aligning solutions with broader societal values and long-term goals. Whether ensuring equitable access to public services, simplifying complex healthcare systems, or embedding transparency in sustainability efforts, UX drives change at both the tactical and strategic levels. As industries grapple with these challenges, UX professionals play a key role in guiding innovation while keeping the focus on human-centered outcomes.

However, this also brings new responsibilities. The more UX influences critical fields, the more ethical considerations come into play. For instance, while AI offers immense opportunities for healthcare and public services, it also presents risks if poorly designed or misaligned with societal values. UX professionals must balance the push for innovation with ensuring systems remain ethical, equitable, and sustainable. This responsibility aligns with the "planet-centric design" and ethical AI trends discussed in Chapter 13, reinforcing that UX professionals are stewards of user and societal well-being.

As we look to the future, one thing is clear: UX must transcend traditional boundaries to address deeply rooted and interconnected challenges. It is not just about making technology easier to use but about designing empathetic, inclusive, and impactful systems. By embracing this responsibility, UX professionals can lead the way in creating solutions that meet user needs and align with societal and environmental values.

In the next chapter, we asked our Titans for their secret UX tips. Let us find out what they had to say.

15

Psst … here are our Titan's secret tips

Chapter fifteen

Psst ... here are our Titan's secret tips

15.1 What to expect from this chapter

We asked our UX Titans: "Is there a secret UX tip you want to share with others?" Their answers reveal not one hidden formula but a collection of practical insights that guide their work and mindset.

In this chapter, you'll discover why empathy is more than a buzzword, how curiosity fuels progress, and why it pays to challenge your own assumptions. You'll learn how documenting your work can amplify your impact, how aligning UX with business goals builds trust and influence, and how networking can open unexpected doors. Our Titans also reflect on the importance of courage, honesty, and the often-overlooked value of simply staying persistent.

15.2 Use empathy to see through other's eyes.

Among the many insights shared by the Titans, one theme emerged with striking consistency: empathy. Good UX often begins with empathy for users, but it does not stop at the user.

Whether working with teammates, stakeholders, or even clients unfamiliar with design, empathy is the thread that weaves everything together.

For Uwe Betzin, this means adopting the language of the person you speak to. "It's better," he suggests, "to avoid words like 'design' entirely when you're in a product discussion. Instead, try speaking their language. Use the words they're comfortable with. You'll find they're more receptive, and you'll make your point more effectively."

This idea of tailoring communication extends into the very questions we ask. Marc Hassenzahl frames it as a shift from "how" and "what" to "why." For him, the art of UX lies in understanding deeper motivations. "Why might an older person use Skype? It's not because they crave modern technology; they want to connect with distant grandchildren." By focusing on this emotional driver, Marc Hassenzahl advocates designing inherently more human solutions, even if they do not always yield immediate commercial success. The why question, he argues, "is critical to creating meaningful products."

Empathy also requires UXers to see their work through the eyes of someone unfamiliar with it. Lutz Krauß explains: "Imagine your mother or partner using the system. Would it make sense to them? What if they weren't tech-savvy? Would they find it intuitive, or would they struggle?" He continues, "The goal is to step out of your expert mindset and consider the experience as a complete outsider. It's a simple exercise, yet it often reveals blind spots in even the most polished designs."

Sarah Diefenbach builds on this by emphasizing the importance of clarity. How much information does a user truly need? How many options should they face at any given moment? "Good UX," she explains, "requires us to be conscious of what people might misinterpret and to design in a way that makes their path as straightforward as possible. To explore that, you need empathy."

15.3 Be open, be curious, and do not fall in love with your work.

In the ever-evolving UX landscape, an open and curious mindset is not just an advantage; it is essential. Our Titans mentioned already that on different occasions throughout the book. When asked for their secret tips, it is mentioned again:

"Never stop questioning," Tobias Oberpaul advises, adding an important caveat: "Balance exploration with efficiency. Don't fall into perfectionism, but always strive for better solutions."

Oliver Kulpi looks at the question from a different angle. He says: "Unlearning what you've learned is very important. You must forget preconceived notions to approach new ideas with neutrality. It's not easy, but it's necessary." For Oliver Kulpi, this unlearning act allows him to stay curious and empathize with users from different backgrounds or age groups without interference from bias or past knowledge. He likens it to becoming "an empty barrel," open to being filled with new insights and experiences. This mindset is especially crucial in emerging trends, such as generative AI, where past processes may no longer apply.

For Nis Boy Naeve, curiosity takes a similar form. "Trust no one, especially not yourself," he says, with a hint of humor that underscores a more profound truth. "Validate assumptions and maintain a healthy skepticism to ensure you're on the right path." Even when working with others with similar perspectives, validating assumptions and challenging collective biases is vital. Nis Boy Naeve stresses the importance of questioning whether a problem is fully understood or whether the team's approach remains sound. This does not mean indulging in negativity or distrust but cultivating a "healthy mistrust" that encourages ongoing reflection. In his view, a curious mindset is not about doubting for its own sake but about staying grounded, open, and flexible enough to pivot when necessary.

Kevin Liang expands on this mindset: "One secret UX tip is that I think imposter syndrome[39] works. If people have imposter syndrome, they treat things as drafts or works in progress and get feedback." His advice encourages designers "not to fall in love with their work. By treating designs as drafts rather than finished masterpieces, UX professionals stay humble, open to feedback, and willing to iterate toward better solutions".

These insights reveal a powerful combination: staying curious, questioning assumptions, and avoiding attachment to your work. Cultivating this balance in a field that requires constant growth and iteration helps UX professionals navigate complexity.

[39] Imposter syndrome refers to the feeling of self-doubt or inadequacy despite evident success, where individuals fear being exposed as a "fraud" even when they are competent and capable.

15.4 Network as much as possible

If empathy is the heart of UX, then networking is its engine. According to four Titans, connecting with others through mentorship, collaboration, or shared experiences is invaluable, particularly for those just starting.

Bill Albert credits much of his growth to moments of connection. Reflecting on his career, he recalls: "When you're starting out, attend a conference, introduce yourself, and engage with the community. Though outside your comfort zone, these moments can transform your thinking and open doors."

But beyond personal gain, networking is also about giving back. He notes: "It's not just about what you learn; it's about contributing to the community in return."

Ulf Schubert takes this a step further, highlighting the importance of mentorship. He encourages newcomers to "actively seek out mentors who can guide [them] through the early challenges of the profession." These relationships, he argues, do "not need to last forever. Instead, they serve as waypoints, temporary but crucial connections that provide clarity and direction when needed." And it is not just beginners who benefit. "Even experienced UX professionals," he says, "can gain so much by mentoring others and staying connected to the fresh perspectives that young designers bring."

Dominique Winter echoes this: "I can't point to a single book or resource that changed everything for me," he admits. "But exchanging ideas with peers? That's always been transformative. It's one of the best things you can do."

15.5 Always know what you can contribute to the company's success.

In Chapter 6, the Titans have already clarified that linking UX to business goals is important. In this section, the Titans argue more on a personal level:

Understanding how your work contributes to your organization's goals clarifies your role within the company. It strengthens your ability to advocate for UX and secure the resources you need to be effective.

Thomas Vöhringer-Kuhnt highlights: "From the outset, think about your contribution to the company's success. [...] Communicating this early makes gaining resources and aligning with stakeholders easier." This alignment often requires UX professionals to step outside their comfort zone, as Dominique Winter explains. "Learn the language of product managers and stakeholders. Understanding their world lets you communicate and collaborate effectively." Whether it is mastering concepts in finance, technology, or marketing, this fluency allows UX practitioners to frame their contributions in ways that resonate with their audience.

However, showing your value is not just about communication – it is also about engagement. Matthias Schulz highlights: "Your early involvement helps other team members lose their fears and understand what UX achieves. [...] Even a small workshop or a few user interviews can show how UX immediately adds value. Team members realize it's not extra work – it's just a different, smarter way of working." Gabriela Gomes adds: "It's about using your resources wisely and not getting carried away by the possibilities. Understand what will deliver the most value and focus on that."

By aligning your work with organizational objectives, engaging teams early, and communicating its value, you establish yourself as a strategic partner in the company's success. This approach not only garners trust in you but also ensures that UX is generally seen as a driver of business success rather than an isolated function.

15.6 Document and pass on the knowledge gained.

In UX, documentation often feels like an afterthought. Yet, during the book, our Titans already stated that documentation is vital to learning as a company.

Carmen Fehrenbach repeats this as one of her secret tips: "Document and tell the story of what you've done. That always falls behind us because it doesn't pay into anything immediately." While it may seem like "mopping up," she insists it is "a vital practice that preserves insights and demonstrates the value of UX." Carmen advocates for even simple steps: "For everything you've done, produce a one-slider somehow, so you can see a bit of what you've achieved over the years and tell others about it." This benefits the individual, acting as a portfolio of achievements, and builds enthusiasm for UX by highlighting the difference between "what's it like with UX and without UX."

For Carmen, documentation is about capturing the past and shaping the future. It elevates UX practice by turning each project into a learning experience, building a foundation for others to grow from, and improving the field.

15.7 Master courage and perseverance

As three of our Titans emphasize, great design requires bold decisions, persistence, and the ability to act despite uncertain outcomes. For Kerstin Dyck, courage is about stepping away from too much caution and embracing action at the right time instead of feeling unable to go on due to many unknowns. She observes: "If you mess up, it all goes away eventually, or you fix it in the next iteration, and you have learned from it. It's better to be bold than to stay too cautious and mediocre." She suggests: "When you deal with a reversible decision, failure is temporary – it passes." What matters is daring to try rather than getting stuck in mediocrity through caution.

Gabriela Gomes adds another dimension: "Maybe related to that too, the other secret is having ideas is very easy. You're not that special. Everyone has ideas, but the ability to follow through and see if that will work, to iterate, and to implement it is what really counts, and that is a messy process. Therefore, cool ideas will not take you that far if it's just that." For Gabriela, the real measure of success lies not in generating ideas but in the perseverance to iterate and bring them to life.

In the iteration process, rejection is a reality of UX work, but it does not have to be a dead end. Katja Busch encourages a shift in mindset: "If something gets in your way, turn the perspective around. Ask, 'What are the benefits here? Why is this situation good?' Context analysis from different perspectives takes the pressure off you as a UXer. It helps you see solutions instead of problems." For Katja, this reframing is about problem-solving and staying adaptable.

Courage in UX is about embracing uncertainty, acting boldly, and staying determined to follow through. It means reframing challenges, accepting setbacks as temporary, and turning ideas into reality through perseverance and iteration.

15.8 There are no secret tips; UX is transparent.

Despite the aura of mystery that sometimes surrounds UX, some of our Titans emphasize that there are no hidden secrets. Gert-Dieter Tuzar humorously states: "Nothing is secret. It's not some dark art. You just have to do it. You need a bit of know-how, but there's nothing hidden. There's no great guru who knows how it's done. No – it's accessible to anyone with the right mindset and skills. It's all transparent, all in the light, not the shadows." For Gert-Dieter Tuzar, UX is about putting in the work and continuously learning rather than searching for shortcuts or exclusive tips.

Dominique Winter reinforces this perspective: "The UX secret tip? I don't have any secret tips. They're all well-known." He suggests UX is built on shared knowledge and widely available practices. "There's no insider magic – just openness, curiosity, and a commitment to improving through experience."

For these Titans, the transparency of UX is its strength. Anyone with the right mindset, skills, and willingness to engage with the work can succeed.

15.9 Summary

Most Titans agree that no single tip will revolutionize UX work. Instead, success lies in combining many small practices that make work easier, more impactful, and more successful. Here is the complete list of tips shared by our Titans:

- **Use empathy to see through other's eyes:** Empathy is the foundation of great UX work. By understanding the goals, perspectives, and language of others, you build stronger connections and create more human-centered solutions.
- **Be open, be curious, and do not fall in love with your work:** Cultivate curiosity by questioning assumptions, unlearning preconceived notions, and treating every design as a work in progress. Staying open to feedback ensures continuous growth and improvement.
- **Network as much as possible:** Build connections within the UX community through mentorship, collaboration, and knowledge exchange. Networking inspires growth, whether you are just starting or are an experienced professional.
- **Always know what you can contribute to the company's success:** Align your UX work with organizational goals, communicate its value clearly, and demonstrate impact. Understanding your role helps you secure support and resources.
- **Document and pass on the knowledge gained:** Preserve insights and share learnings to advance your growth and the UX field. Simple documentation can build enthusiasm for UX and demonstrate its value over time.

- **Master courage and perseverance:** Embrace challenges, reframe setbacks as opportunities, and follow through on ideas. Persistence and bold action turn concepts into impactful outcomes.
- **There are no secret tips; UX is transparent:** Success in UX comes from openness, sharing knowledge, and committing to the work. There is no hidden magic – just continuous learning, iteration, and improvement.

15.10 Our thoughts

At its core, UX is a deeply human business. Success often depends on the collaboration of diverse disciplines, such as software developers, designers, and UX researchers, all working toward a shared goal. Each discipline brings unique expertise, but true greatness comes only when everyone accepts that the best results are achieved together. Reflecting on the tips shared by our Titans, we see this idea echoed repeatedly: empathy, networking, and sharing knowledge are key ingredients for fostering collaboration between users, teammates, stakeholders, and clients. Without it, even the most skilled teams risk failing to create meaningful, impactful user experiences.

This connection between empathy, networking, and sharing knowledge extends beyond product development into the broader business context. Many of our Titans highlighted the importance of always knowing how to contribute to the company's goals. Creating a brilliant product is one part of the equation, but for it to succeed, it must also resonate in the marketplace. Business success ensures the product can spread, reach more users, and improve lives.

We have experienced firsthand the consequences of neglecting this balance. A pipette manufacturer once approached us for a UX test with their newly developed pipette. The goal was to showcase its superiority over competitors and make usability the centerpiece of its marketing. The team had poured years into perfecting the technical aspects of the product. However, when we conducted the tests, the results were stark: while the pipette was technically flawless, it failed to meet users' expectations. It was considered awkward to handle, and a wide margin preferred competitors' products. Despite the technical achievements, the product was never brought to market, and years of development were ultimately abandoned. In this case, the engineers fell in love with their product, ignoring everything besides the technology. This is a powerful reminder: technical perfection alone cannot guarantee success – it must be paired with a deep understanding of user needs and market demands.

We could tell similar stories with teams focusing exclusively on design, UX, or any discipline. Only the interplay of these perspectives – technical, design, business, and UX – creates products capable of thriving in today's complex world and ultimately reaching the company's goals. And like our Titans said in their tips, this interplay needs communication across all disciplines.

We want to bring another example that resonates with the Titan's tip to master courage and perseverance. In our agency work, we have encountered situations where clients sought to "buy testing results," – such as a software company wanting us to validate their work to impress their clients. This is where one of our agency's guiding principles, "The data is sacred," becomes critical. We consistently refuse to compromise our integrity, ensuring that our findings reflect reality rather than convenience. Staying firm in such moments requires courage to challenge expectations and perseverance to uphold the standards we believe in, even when it might mean losing a project or even a customer. This stance aligns with the Titans' wisdom: mastering courage and perseverance allows UX professionals to navigate difficult situations with integrity, building trust and credibility.

The next chapter delves into what our Titans would like to learn next. From mastering new tools to exploring emerging technologies, they reveal how curiosity and growth fuel their success in a constantly evolving field.

16

Learning never ends – what our Titans would like to learn.

Chapter sixteen

Learning never ends – what our Titans would like to learn.

16.1 What to expect from this chapter

Learning is the heartbeat of UX. It drives us to improve, adapt, and stay relevant in an ever-changing field. For our UX Titans, learning never truly ends. Mastering new tools and technologies, exploring more profound research methods, and refining personal skills, curiosity, and growth are essential for success.

In this chapter, our Titans share what they want to learn next. You'll discover how they aim to grow personally by diving into new tools, methods, and technologies like AI. You'll also see how they want to bridge the gap between design and impact – learning skills like coding or ROI analysis to ensure their work makes it into the final product and proves its worth. They'll explore the power of coaching others and reflect on a bold truth: maybe we already have what we need.

16.2 Always growing: The Titan's drive to learn new skills.

They stated it on some occasions in the book, but you could read it everywhere between the lines: Our Titans are lifelong learners, always eager to grow and sharpen their craft. They see personal growth as a way to stay ahead in UX, whether picking up new tools, diving deeper into research, or exploring emerging technologies. Here are some examples of what they're curious about:

Uwe Betzin wants to master a new tool to keep his workflows fresh. He says: "I come from Axure[40] because it was great for complex interactions. I'd actually like to learn Figma[41] – it seems interesting." Lutz Krauß shares a similar drive, looking for tools that match the field's shift toward integrated design: "I think the UX role is shifting from designing interaction flows to more integrated implementation. There are probably tools out there I don't even know exist yet, and I'd like to learn more about that."

Research is another area where Titans want to grow. Uwe Betzin is curious about quantitative methods: "I'd like to get into quantitative research. I've observed it from afar but haven't experienced it closely yet." Gert-Dieter Tuzar agrees, aiming to boost his analytical skills: "I want to get better at statistics." For Dominique Winter, it's about asking better questions: "I think I do good interviews, but deep psychological interviews, really scientific ones – that's something I'd love to learn."

[40] Axure is a UX design and prototyping tool that enables designers to create interactive, high-fidelity wireframes and user flows. It's especially popular for building complex, logic-based prototypes without writing code.

[41] Figma is a collaborative, cloud-based design tool widely used for user interface and user experience (UI/UX) design. It allows teams to design, prototype, and give feedback in real time within the same platform.

Emerging tech, especially AI, also sparks their interest, even if still in the idea phase. Kerstin Dyck pictures AI that measures emotions to deepen user insights: "It would be exciting to measure user emotions better reliably. That's where AI could come in." Guido Meier-Arendt envisions empathetic AI systems: "We need tools that can recognize emotional states and adapt interactions accordingly – like empathic assistants." Uwe Betzin imagines AI transforming usability tests: "A fantastic idea would be semi-moderated usability tests during usage, evaluated by AI."

For our Titans, growth isn't just about keeping up – it's about pushing boundaries, refining skills, and exploring what's next.

16.3 Bridging the Gap: Making UX Work Count

Our Titans don't just want to learn for themselves – they want their work to have a real impact. That means bridging the gap between design, execution, and management, ensuring that products with better UX actually hit the market. Therefore, they're eager to learn skills like coding and "talking ROI" to make that happen.

Some Titans see their coding skills as a way to create better, more feasible UX designs and to communicate them. Gabriela Gomes has already experienced its power: "I'm actually very much back into programming right now. Understanding the technical behavior of things I design enables me to create more informed, technically feasible solutions. I started by making games and learning C#. For me, that was incredible because it really amplified my ability to prototype and communicate ideas." Katja Busch agrees, wanting to understand tech to improve her and her team's work: "I'd like to understand better how technology works on a smaller scale so I can design faster and more effectively with the team." Sarah Diefenbach sees coding as a way to simplify her process: "I think it would be really cool if programming, or handling technology in general, became easier in many areas. This would help improve UX." Matthias Schulz also wants to learn front-end development to align with devs: "I'd like to learn more about design and front-end development, but it would take time and effort, like attending courses."

Others focus on talking ROI to ensure better UX gets the green light. Thomas Vöhringer-Kuhnt wants to get better at discussing business value: "Maybe topics that go in the direction of business economics, like the return on investment we discussed earlier – that's something I'd like to understand better." Dominique Winter also aims to master the language of executives: "I'd like to be more confident in dealing with economic topics like ROI and presenting these to executives." Carmen Fehrenbach even imagines tools for that: "Imagine if there were a machine that could simply calculate the ROI of UI changes. That would make explaining UX so much easier."

For these Titans, learning new skills isn't just about personal growth – it's about ensuring their work leads to better UX in products that make it to market, from concept to reality.

16.4 Coaching UXers: Growing teams, growing yourself

For many of our Titans, learning is not just about improving their skills – it is about helping others grow. Mentoring and coaching colleagues, teams, and the broader UX community allow professionals to share knowledge, build stronger teams, and develop leadership abilities.

Dominique Winter: "I'd like to focus more on coaching – how to better support people on their journey, particularly in UX." For him (and many other Titans), coaching is about offering guidance, helping others find their way, and creating an environment where UX knowledge and skills can flourish. In turn, mentoring others challenges professionals to reflect on their work and sharpen their abilities as communicators and leaders.

In addition, coaching is described as "learning through the process". Helping others navigate their UX journey strengthens team collaboration, promotes shared understanding, and empowers individuals to contribute more effectively. As our Titans show, growing others and growing yourself go hand in hand often.

16.5 The bold truth: We already have what we need

After sharing their ambitions for learning – new tools, advanced research, coding skills, and emerging technologies – our Titans remind us of a powerful truth: we already have the essential knowledge, frameworks, and tools to create exceptional UX. Success does not always require more – it requires doing better with what we already know.

Gert-Dieter Tuzar highlights this reality, emphasizing the importance of action over searching for something new: "Everything needed for success already exists; we just need to act."

Marc Hassenzahl shares a similar sentiment, pointing to UX professionals' foundational knowledge: "We already have everything we need – psychology, methods, and frameworks. It's a matter of doing better work with what we have."

These reflections offer a refreshing perspective in a field that constantly pushes for more tools, trends, and technologies. While growth is essential, true progress comes not from endless searching but from doing. A bold call to action our Titans leave us with.

16.6 Summary

As we saw earlier, learning is not just a task for our Titans – it is a mindset that drives their work and shapes their success. In this chapter, they shared their aspirations for growth, revealing a desire to expand their skills, embrace new tools, and keep up with an ever-changing field.

From exploring new tools like Figma and diving into advanced research methods to experimenting with AI, the Titans showed how personal growth keeps them sharp and ready for what's next. They also focused on bridging the gap – learning coding, visual design, and ROI skills to ensure the UX work makes it into the final product and proves its value to the business.

Learning isn't just about their own skills, though. Several Titans emphasized the importance of coaching and mentoring others – sharing their knowledge, building stronger teams, and growing as leaders.

At the heart of all these ambitions lies a bold and refreshing truth: we already have the tools, methods, and frameworks we need. Our Titans remind us that success comes not from endless searching but from using what we already have to create better, more meaningful work.

16.7 Our thoughts

This chapter shows that our Titans continuously seek to learn new tools, refine research methods, and explore emerging technologies. This relentless drive is what propels UX forward. Yet, it is also a double-edged sword, as some Titans explained. Pursuing the next tool, framework, or skill can sometimes overshadow the opportunity to master and extract full value from what is already available.

We know this from our journey. Before founding our agency over a decade ago, we were university researchers focusing on UX, Usability, and UI. When we started the agency while still working other jobs, we were essentially freelancers with a dream. As our projects grew in scope and we began hiring, we remained deeply rooted in our expert roles. While we built a team, the agency's core was two specialists supported by other "assistant experts." Only in the past few years have we shifted toward a more strategic business focus.

This shift was difficult because the drive to innovate and improve is deeply ingrained in us, like many other UX professionals. We are drawn to "fixing things" or finding "the next big thing." Maintaining and improving something that already works does not ignite the same excitement. And yet, as we have learned, true growth and value often come from sustaining and refining what is already strong.

Reflecting on our Titans' insights, we see a profession that thrives on the belief that "there must be a better way." This mindset not only drives innovation but also extends to the UX workflow itself. The desire to work smarter and deliver better outcomes influences how UXers approach challenges, collaborate with teams, and advocate for users. Even as they ascend to leadership roles, the essence of being a practitioner remains intact – continually questioning, experimenting, and improving.

However, this relentless pursuit of growth brings a critical challenge. There is a risk of prioritizing novelty over mastery. As some Titans observed, UX already has a wealth of tools, methods, and frameworks that can drive impactful solutions if applied systematically and thoughtfully. Balancing the urge to explore new possibilities with a disciplined approach to leveraging proven strategies is key to creating sustainable organizational value.

Ultimately, the insights shared in this chapter highlight an inspiring truth: UXers are perpetual learners driven by curiosity and a commitment to improvement. However, while learning never ends, using what we already know is a huge opportunity. As UX professionals, the challenge is to combine our hunger for growth with the patience and discipline to apply existing tools, practices, and strategies meaningfully. Long-term success lies in this balance – not just for our field but for the users and organizations we aim to serve. Or, as former U.S. President Obama put it in a very different situation: "The value lies in getting shit done."

This concludes the interview section of this book. In the next chapter, we want to help you determine if UX resonates with you and might be your calling (if it isn't already).

17

If you aren't a UXer yet – is it your calling?

Chapter seventeen

If you aren't a UXer yet – is it your calling?

17.1 What to expect from this chapter

As we saw in the book, UX is more than just a profession; it is a mindset, a curiosity for how people interact with the world, and a drive to improve that interaction. This chapter will help you discover if UX might be your calling.

First, we will immerse you in a day in the life of a UX professional. What does it mean to create user experiences? What kinds of challenges, collaborations, and rewards define this work? By stepping into the shoes of a UXer, you will get a glimpse of what the role entails.

Next, we will guide you through reflective questions to help you explore your fit for the profession. Whether your background is in design, technology, psychology, or something entirely different, UX offers a place for diverse talents. We will share how different skills, perspectives, and passions can come together to build great user experiences.

Finally, we will encourage you to take the first steps on your UX journey, emphasizing that there is no single path into the field. Whether you are a curious beginner or an experienced professional considering a transition, UX is about growth, learning, and the desire to make a difference.

17.2 A day in the life of a UX professional

What does it mean to work in UX? While no two days are alike, a typical day for a UX professional involves balancing creativity, collaboration, and problem-solving to shape meaningful user experiences. Here is a glimpse into the dynamic and rewarding world of UX:

Morning: Setting the stage for success

The day might begin with a team meeting to align on goals. UX professionals collaborate with (other) designers, developers, product managers, and stakeholders, ensuring everyone understands the vision. Clarity and alignment are key in designing a new app feature or improving an existing service.

After the meeting, the focus often shifts to planning and analysis. This could mean reviewing usability test results from the previous day, mapping out user journeys, or analyzing behavioral data to uncover patterns. To understand users' needs, motivations, and pain points. If you have already read the book, remember Chapter 15.2, which is called: "Use empathy to see through other's eyes.". That is exactly what you are aiming for here.

Midday: Collaborating and creating

Collaboration is at the heart of UX work. Midday often involves sketching wireframes or prototyping ideas, using tools like Figma or Axure to bring concepts to life. Feedback from team members helps refine designs, ensuring they are both user-friendly and aligned with business goals.

If you are more focused on UX research, you might not be actively using a prototyping tool. Instead, you might do it in a team or focus on preparing the next user test guideline.

This is also a prime time for tackling challenges. Whether balancing user needs with technical constraints or navigating stakeholder priorities, the work requires problem-solving. As Dominique Winter says, "The magic of UX lies in finding that sweet spot where user satisfaction meets business success."

Afternoon: Testing

Testing brings designs to life. It involves conducting usability tests or observing users interact with prototypes. Feedback from these sessions informs the next iteration of the design, ensuring it is intuitive and effective. Workshops or stakeholder presentations might also occur, allowing for alignment and fresh perspectives.

End of business: Reflecting and Learning

As the day winds down, reflection is key. UXers take time to assess what went well and identify areas for improvement. Some explore emerging UX trends, experiment with tools, or engage with peers in the community.

Because UX is a constantly evolving field, growth never stops. As Gabriela Gomes said, "UX isn't about being perfect – it's about staying curious and committed to growth."

A note on the pace of UX work

The day we have described offers a glimpse into the dynamic nature of UX work, but it is worth noting that the pace can vary depending on the company, project, and team structure. In some organizations, what happens in a single day here might unfold over a week, a month – or even longer. The essence, however, remains the same: balancing creativity, collaboration, and user focus to design impactful experiences.

17.3 Questions to ask yourself: Could UX be for you?

If a day in the life of a UX professional resonated with you, it is time to dive in deeper. UX is a diverse field that welcomes people from various backgrounds but also requires a specific mindset and skills. Inspired by our Titans' experiences, the following reflective questions can help you determine if UX might be your calling.

Be aware: These questions are not a checklist to prove you are ready for UX. Instead, they are an opportunity to reflect on your interests, values, and aspirations. There is no one-size-fits-all path into UX; no one starts with all the answers. If these questions spark excitement or curiosity, UX could be a journey worth exploring.

Do you have a natural curiosity about people and their experiences?

UX starts with understanding users' motivations, behaviors, and pain points. Marc Hassenzahl captured this beautifully in Chapter 7: " Rather than asking users what they dislike, we focus on what they love. When did they enjoy a train journey, for instance?

Understanding these positive moments lets us create experiences that others can enjoy." If you are fascinated by what drives human behavior, UX could be a place to thrive.

Do you enjoy solving problems in creative and practical ways?
UX requires striking the right balance between ingenuity and pragmatism. Oliver Kulpi noted in Chapter 15, "Unlearning what you've learned is very important. You must forget preconceived notions to approach new ideas with neutrality." The ability to think outside the box while staying grounded in real-world constraints defines a great UX professional.

Do you like collaboration?
In UX, collaboration is not optional – it is essential. UXers work closely with designers, developers, business stakeholders, and users to co-create the best solutions. If you find energy in teamwork and enjoy learning from others, this is a profession where you will fit in naturally.

Are you adaptable and willing to grow?
UX is a dynamic field that constantly evolves. Staying curious, learning new tools, and adapting to emerging trends is part of the job. UX will keep you engaged and challenged if you are open to continuous learning.

Do you embrace feedback and iteration?
No design is perfect on the first try. UX involves cycles of testing, feedback, and refinement. Kevin Liang's advice in Chapter 15 reminds us: "By treating designs as drafts rather than finished

masterpieces, UX professionals stay humble, open to feedback, and willing to iterate toward better solutions." UX offers endless growth opportunities if you enjoy learning from feedback and improving your work.

17.4 Your Journey Awaits

UX is not about being perfect but about curiosity, empathy, and the drive to make a difference. It is a field that celebrates diversity in thought, background, and approach, where the goal is not to check every box but to keep growing, learning, and improving.

If this chapter has sparked your interest, consider taking the next step. Dive deeper into UX through courses or books, join local or online communities to connect with like-minded professionals, or experiment with tools and techniques. Whether you are sketching user journeys, building prototypes, or analyzing user behavior, every step is a step forward.

Remember, there is no singular path to becoming a UX professional. Some enter from design, others from psychology, technology, business, or completely different fields – each brings a unique perspective that strengthens the field.

So, embrace the journey ahead. UX is not a destination but an ongoing exploration of what it means to create meaningful experiences. The possibilities are endless, with curiosity as your compass and empathy as your guide. Your journey in UX awaits – and we'd love to be part of it.

Hint: If you are preparing to apply for a job, there is a list of questions you could use to prepare in the bonus material of this

Early Buyer Edition of UX Titans. You can download it here: www.uxtitans.com/early-buyer-edition

We would also love to connect with you:
https://www.linkedin.com/in/dr-benjamin-franz/
https://www.linkedin.com/in/dr-michaela-kauer-franz/

We can't wait to see what you create.

18

Get to know our UX Titans.

Chapter eighteen

Get to know our UX Titans.

This chapter will introduce all our Titans in depth and with the space they deserve. When we started this book project, one of the first things we discussed was how to choose our Titans. Coming from an academic background, we felt the need for some rules.

As you can imagine, the field of UX is big and ever-growing. Therefore, the list is not meant to be "final." We hope to expand our network in the future and integrate more insights from more Titans worldwide. If you know some, please let us know and suggest a Titan under www.uxtitans.com

But now, without further ado. Here are the rules we used to select our UX Titans:

- **Coming from the Industry:** Titans coming from the industry must either work for companies with more than 1000 people and have a transformational role there, or they must be consulting companies that develop products for millions of people.

- **Coming from academia:** Titans coming from academia must have published work that more than 1000 peers have cited. Ensuring that their influence is far-reaching within the academic field.
- **Public persons in UX:** Titans, active as speakers and trainers, must have a followership of more than 1000 people on their social media accounts. The social media accounts need to focus on UX to be counted. This ensures that everything they say is heard by various people, making them a multiplier in the field and shaping it directly.

And now, it is time to meet our Titans.

18.1 Bill Albert

Dr. Bill Albert is a trailblazer in UX design, product innovation, and strategic consulting. With over two decades of pioneering contributions, he has cemented his reputation as a thought leader who bridges the gap between groundbreaking research and practical application. As the founder and principal of Greenlight Idea Lab, Bill spearheads an agency uniquely focused on measuring and validating product desirability, leveraging proprietary methodologies to ensure innovation teams achieve exceptional product-market fit.

Bill Albert's illustrious career includes key leadership roles, such as Executive Director of Bentley University's User Experience Center, where he established a globally recognized hub for UX research and education, generating over $1M annually. At Mach49, he led a global team of UX professionals, driving innovation by integrating AI into customer insights and championing mixed-methods research to validate new ventures. His tenure at Fidelity Investments saw the transformation of digital financial tools for millions of users, underscoring his ability to deliver scalable, impactful solutions.

Beyond his professional accomplishments, Bill Albert has made significant academic contributions, including co-authoring seminal books like "Measuring the User Experience," publishing numerous peer-reviewed articles, and serving as Co-Editor-in-Chief of the Journal of User Experience. His work has shaped industry standards, introducing innovative UX metrics and research methods that continue to influence practitioners worldwide.

A seasoned mentor and speaker, Bill Albert's legacy lies in his unmatched ability to inspire teams, foster inclusive leadership, and craft user experiences that balance empathy with data-driven precision. His commitment to improving lives through design has earned him a place among the Titans of the UX field.

18.2 Carmen Fehrenbach

Carmen Fehrenbach is a recognized leader in the field of user experience, boasting an impressive career that spans over two decades. As a Manager of UX at Deutsche Telekom, she has dedicated the last 11+ years to crafting innovative, user-centered digital experiences at one of Europe's leading telecom companies. Her expertise extends far beyond interface design, encompassing end-to-end user research, design thinking facilitation, and the cultivation of cutting-edge UX methodologies.

Carmen Fehrenbach's journey in UX began with her foundational work as a usability engineer and researcher at companies like SAP and User Interface Design GmbH. At SapientNitro, she advanced to the role of Senior Information Architect, where she honed her skills in managing user requirements, prototyping, and usability testing while navigating complex client relations. Over her career, Carmen Fehrenbach has amassed deep expertise in interaction design, heuristic evaluation, wireframing, and contextual inquiry, making her a sought-after voice in the UX community.

In the last few years, she has also taken over the role of Epic Owner Accessibility at Deutsche Telekom. In this role, she focuses on bringing UX to customer groups that have not been adequately considered in the past: people with impairments.

What makes her a true Titan in the field of UX is her unwavering dedication to the principles of user-centered design, combined with a track record of tangible impact. Whether through leading complex UX projects at Deutsche Telekom or mentoring teams to push the boundaries of design innovation, Carmen Fehrenbach continues to shape the future of digital experiences, ensuring technology serves humanity at its best.

18.3 Dominique Winter

With an extensive background in coaching, consulting, and hands-on product development, this expert has established himself as a true Titan in the field of UX. Based in Düsseldorf, Germany, his work is centered around helping organizations and product teams harness the full potential of user experience to drive success. His approach transcends traditional UX methodologies, focusing on creating meaningful experiences that resonate with users while elevating product effectiveness.

Over the years, Dominique Winter has worked with major companies such as OBI Group Holding and REWE Digital, where he coached Product Owners and Product Managers, led transformative workshops, and integrated user-centered design into every stage of the product lifecycle. His leadership in creating strong product visions and aligning teams around a shared understanding of user needs has helped countless organizations craft experiences that engage and delight users.

In addition to his corporate success, Dominique Winter is an accomplished speaker and content creator, offering valuable insights through podcasts, workshops, and training sessions for product leaders across various industries. He uniquely can blend theoretical knowledge with practical, experience-driven strategies, fostering a culture of continuous improvement and organizational development.

A true advocate for the power of UX in product development, his work reflects a deep commitment to making products usable and transforming them into experiences that users remember and cherish. By coaching, mentoring, and guiding teams, Dominique Winter continues to push the boundaries of what great UX can achieve, making him a defining force in the industry.

18.4 Gabriela Gomes

Gabriela Purri R. Gomes is a pioneering force in the field of UX design, renowned for her multidisciplinary approach that blends human-centered product design, storytelling, and innovation. With over a decade of experience, she has made significant contributions across diverse industries, including digital technology, telecommunications, healthcare, and entertainment. Her expertise spans human-computer interaction, software development, and inclusive design, areas where she has continually pushed boundaries to create more equitable and accessible technological futures.

Gabriela Gomes's career trajectory is defined by her leadership roles in prestigious organizations such as Deutsche Telekom, where she drives digital product development and innovation. In academia, she was an Annenberg Fellow at the USC Game Innovation Lab and a Visiting Scholar at USC's Creative Media & Behavioral Health Center, contributing to projects at the intersection of media, technology, and health. Her work extends beyond design into the realm of research and development, where she has led transformative projects that integrate the latest advancements in human-computer interaction, IoT, and immersive environments.

Her impact is global, with her work recognized at top international publications and festivals like the Tokyo Game Show, OpenIDEO, and the Association for Computing Machinery (ACM). Whether designing award-winning products for older adults with dementia or leading cross-disciplinary teams to tackle complex challenges, Gabriela Gomes's dedication to human-centered design is evident. She keeps users' lived experiences and diverse needs at the core of every project, ensuring her solutions are innovative but also meaningful and inclusive.

Her deep knowledge, strategic leadership, and passion for creating a more inclusive technological landscape establish her firmly as a UX Titan, shaping the future of product and experience design across the globe.

18.5 Gert-Dieter Tuzar

Gert-Dieter Tuzar is a Senior Expert in UX and Human-Machine Interaction (HMI) with over 30 years of experience in the automotive and technology sectors. His career includes significant roles at companies like Faurecia, Visteon Electronics, Johnson Controls Automotive, and Siemens VDO, where he has driven the design of innovative user interfaces for complex systems.

Gert-Dieter Tuzar holds a Master's degree in Design Development and Cognitive Systems Engineering from The Ohio State University and a Dipl. Des. in Industrial Design from Hochschule Pforzheim. His deep expertise in HMI design and his ability to blend human-centered design with cutting-edge technology make him a standout figure in the UX field.

At Faurecia, Gert-Dieter Tuzar continues to lead the development of advanced, user-focused designs that enhance safety and usability in automotive environments, solidifying his reputation as a UX Titan.

18.6 Guido Meier-Arendt

Guido Meier-Arendt is a pioneering Human-Machine Interaction (HMI) expert with over two decades of experience driving automotive and user-centered design innovations. At the time of the interview, he was serving as an HMI Expert at Continental AG, where he cemented his reputation as a thought leader in developing intuitive, adaptive interfaces for modern vehicles. His career spans academia and industry, bridging theoretical foundations with real-world applications to improve the user experience, particularly in automated and assisted driving technologies.

With a rich history of collaboration with leading automotive companies like Siemens VDO, Guido Meier-Arendt has authored numerous influential publications that delve into the ergonomics, functionality, and usability of HMI systems. His contributions, including groundbreaking work on advanced driver assistance systems (ADAS) and the future of automated driving, reflect his deep understanding of the complex relationship between technology and human behavior. His research on adaptive, multimodal vehicle interfaces continues to shape the evolution of safer, more intuitive user experiences.

As an innovator and mentor, Guido Meier-Arendt has developed innovative technologies and shaped methodologies that place the user at the heart of design. His ability to integrate interdisciplinary knowledge with real-world usability makes him a true Titan in the UX field, particularly in the rapidly advancing sector of automotive HMI. His work continues to influence the academic and industrial landscapes, driving the future of human-centered design in increasingly autonomous environments.

18.7 Katja Busch

Katja Busch is a pioneering force in the world of UX, blending her deep expertise in digital transformation with a profound understanding of human-centered design. As a business consultant, coach, trainer, and author, she has spent more than a decade at the forefront of shaping user experience strategies, leveraging agile methodologies and artificial intelligence to enhance UX efficiency and innovation.

Katja Busch's journey started with pioneering digital transformation initiatives as an early innovator in multimedia production and digital marketing before advancing to leadership roles. Her focus on UX has been a constant thread throughout her career, from her tenure as Head of User Experience at SapientNitro to Head of Digital Marketing & UX at Vaillant. She later took on complex consulting roles as interim project or product manager. She continued to shape the future of UX training, including as Lead UX Coach at XDi - Experience Design Institute and the future skills department of Haufe Akademie.

At attention.works, her consultancy company, Katja Busch, combines her passion for human-centered innovation with a deep knowledge of digital transformation, neuroscience, and change management. She offers consulting, personal and team coaching, problem-solving workshops, and individual training. Her work spans various industries and company sizes. A key differentiator is the consistent focus of UX methods and tools on the business rather than just the user, customer, or employee experience.

Katja Busch has contributed to the academic field as a sought-after speaker and educator. She is a guest lecturer and author, sharing her UX strategy and innovation expertise with a wider audience. Her impact is felt not only in the organizations she works with but also in the future of UX, where she continues to be a guiding light for businesses striving to balance structure, efficiency, and empathy.

Her blend of leadership, innovation, and human touch makes Katja Busch a true Titan in the UX field, consistently advancing the boundaries of the experience business while prioritizing the human element and opportunities for change at its core.

18.8 Kerstin Dyck

Kerstin Dyck is a trailblazer in the world of UX design, with an impressive career spanning over 17 years. After many years in a UX agency, she works as UX Lead at BTP Design, SAP. She aims to bring together user experience design, service design, and sustainability in her work. Her ability to craft innovative, intuitive, and resource-efficient solutions sets her apart as a true leader in the field. With a strong academic foundation in psychology, Kerstin Dyck approaches every project with a deep commitment to user research, ensuring that the subtleties of user needs and requirements are at the heart of her designs. This dedication enables her to create functional, meaningful, and value-adding products and services.

Throughout her career, Kerstin Dyck has demonstrated exceptional leadership capabilities. She has successfully managed teams and budgets, fostering environments where innovation thrives. At UID GmbH, she held pivotal roles, such as Lead UX and Team Manager, where she sharpened her UX strategy and data visualization expertise. Her work reflects a profound understanding of a systemic design perspective and the importance of integrating sustainability into every aspect of user experience. Kerstin Dyck's ability to align business objectives with user needs has consistently resulted in transformative outcomes for users and organizations.

Her interests extend beyond traditional UX boundaries, encompassing systemic design, sustainable UX, and new work methodologies. She is passionate about creating designs that enhance the quality of life while minimizing resource consumption. Her visionary approach and commitment to pushing the boundaries of what UX can achieve mark her as a Titan in the industry, influencing the present and future of user experience design.

18.9 Kevin Liang

Kevin Liang is a standout figure in the UX field, widely regarded as a UX research Titan, educator, and creator. With over 14 years of behavioral research experience, Kevin has made significant contributions across startup environments and Fortune 500 companies. His expertise spans software and hardware development, and he has co-founded research methods that have influenced significant projects in leading tech companies such as Google and Volkswagen. As a co-inventor of multiple patents, his work has contributed directly to advancements in UX design, particularly in wearable tech and autonomous vehicles.

However, Kevin Liang's role as a mentor and educator truly sets him apart. Through his "Zero to UX" Research Masterclass (zerotoux.com), he has trained and empowered hundreds of aspiring UX researchers, helping them develop the hard and soft skills needed to become leaders in the field. His holistic teaching approach covers research methods, leadership, business strategy, and communication, providing students with the tools to succeed in top-tier companies. His YouTube channel, which quickly became a leader in UX research content, continues to serve a growing community of over 28,000 subscribers, showcasing his ability to engage and educate through digital platforms.

Through his work, Kevin Liang exemplifies what it means to be a true UX Titan – combining expertise, innovation, and a commitment to shaping the next generation of UX leaders. His contributions to the field are both practical and transformative, making him a driving force in the evolution of UX research and education.

18.10 Lutz Krauß

Dr. Lutz W.H. Krauß is a renowned Titan in the field of UX, boasting a distinguished career of over two decades at Porsche AG. His expertise spans human-machine interaction, app development, and UI/UX design, and his work has significantly influenced the evolution of automotive user experiences. Beginning his journey at Porsche in 2003, Lutz Krauß spent 18 years as Head of HMI and UI/UX Display and Operation, spearheading the development of cutting-edge interfaces that seamlessly integrate technology, design, and user needs. In these roles, he focused on creating intuitive and engaging interactions that enhance the driving experience while aligning with Porsche's commitment to innovation and quality.

Since 2021, he has served as Internal Customer Success Lead, where his role extends beyond traditional UX boundaries. He ensures the satisfaction and success of three vital customer groups: end-users, internal collaborators, and stakeholders. This holistic approach highlights his visionary leadership in fostering collaboration and addressing diverse needs across the development process. His ability to align internal teams and stakeholders around user-centered goals has been pivotal in shaping successful, innovative outcomes.

Lutz Krauß's contributions to UX are characterized by his dedication to simplifying complexity and making cutting-edge technology accessible and enjoyable for users. His deep understanding of design, technical proficiency, and strategic thinking have made him a guiding force at Porsche and a trailblazer in the automotive UX industry. These qualities firmly establish him as a Titan whose influence extends beyond his remarkable Porsche career.

18.11 Marc Hassenzahl

Marc Hassenzahl is a distinguished figure in the world of UX, currently serving as a professor for Ubiquitous Design and Experience & Interaction at the University of Siegen, Germany. With a Ph.D. in Psychology from the Technical University of Darmstadt, he has an extensive academic and professional career. His journey includes pioneering research and teaching roles at institutions like the Folkwang University of Arts and the University of Koblenz-Landau, where he laid the groundwork for his research on designing pleasurable and meaningful interactive technologies.

Marc Hassenzahl's career spans academia and industry, with influential roles at Siemens and as a Senior Usability Consultant at User Interface Design GmbH. His leadership in UX research has shaped key theoretical and practical approaches to experience and interaction design. His academic endeavors are complemented by his role as a board member of the German UPA, where he contributed to advancing usability standards.

He has shaped the field of experience design through his groundbreaking research and impacted the way interactive technologies are conceived and developed. His unique blend of psychological insight and design expertise has set the stage for a deeper understanding of user experiences, making him a true thought leader and innovator in UX.

18.12 Matthias Schulz

Matthias Schulz is a Senior UX Strategist and UX Researcher with a diverse background in psychology, design, and computer science. Currently leading UX efforts at Porsche AG, he plays a key role in establishing shared service UX teams and integrating UX practices into agile frameworks like SAFe. Matthias specializes in driving sustainable UX maturity within organizations by developing strategies and defining measurable goals. His expertise also includes evaluating interactive technologies and understanding user contexts, which form the foundation of his approach to creating impactful, user-centered designs.

With over a decade of experience, including a notable tenure at Mercedes-Benz Group AG, Matthias Schulz has consistently demonstrated leadership in UX research and strategy. He has developed and implemented UX studies, guided IT product teams through UX awareness training, and supported executive-level decisions on UX methods. His work extends beyond corporate environments, as he is also a dedicated lecturer at the Hochschule für Technik Stuttgart, where he imparts his knowledge of usability and consumer research to the next generation of UX professionals.

Matthias Schulz's contributions to the field are further evidenced by his extensive involvement in the UX community, from his hands-on work with UX measurement tools to his commitment to advancing agile UX methodologies. His leadership in UX strategy and his deep understanding of human-technology relationships make him a true Titan in the field – constantly pushing the boundaries of what's possible in user experience design.

18.13 Nis Boy Naeve

Nis Boy Naeve stands as a Titan in the field of UX, with an illustrious career spanning nearly three decades at SAP AG. Currently serving as Chief Product Officer (CPO) and Vice President (VP) at SAP, Nis Boy has been a driving force behind the evolution of User Interface (UI) and User Experience (UX) technologies. His strategic oversight and deep expertise in defining and implementing SAP's UI strategy have shaped the company's user-centered design direction.

Nis Boy Naeve's tenure at SAP began in 1995, and since then, he has held various leadership positions. He has led cross-program initiatives, managed UI governance, and developed SAP's key UI frameworks. His work is defined by a pragmatic, goal-oriented approach, following lean principles to enhance user productivity. As CPO and VP, he plays a central role in shaping the future of SAP's UX offerings, creating an enduring impact on both product development and the broader enterprise software landscape.

With a robust foundation in both development and strategic leadership, Nis Boy Naeve has earned recognition as one of the foremost authorities in UX, driving innovations that prioritize user-centricity while maintaining high standards of operational excellence. His contributions have influenced SAP's UX journey and set benchmarks for the industry, solidifying his position as a true UX Titan.

18.14 Oliver Kulpi

Oliver Kulpi is a leading figure in experience design, with over 25 years of expertise spanning multiple industries, including automotive, healthcare, luxury, retail, and transportation. He is the Co-CEO of Digital Experiences Group, Managing Director of Ergosign GmbH, and a Board Member for Ergosign Switzerland AG. His work has involved leading global design teams across Europe, India, and the Asia Pacific region, delivering cutting-edge solutions for enterprise and digital marketing. Oliver Kulpi is an expert in user research, ideation, information architecture, and user-centered design, strongly focusing on digital transformation and innovative tools for design sprints and agile methodologies.

Oliver Kulpi has played a pivotal role in shaping user experience strategies for renowned international car brands, global luxury brands, and leading companies in B2B and healthcare. His leadership in organizations like Valtech, Publicis Sapient, and BMW Group has demonstrated his capacity to manage large-scale projects and teams, consistently delivering innovative and impactful results. Oliver Kulpi is also a certified SAFe Agilist and Scrum Master, underscoring his commitment to agile principles and their application in UX design.

His career trajectory, marked by leadership roles and a deep understanding of cross-functional collaboration, positions him as a Titan in the UX field. His expertise and vision in driving digital transformation make him an invaluable contributor to the future of experience design.

18.15 Sarah Diefenbach

Prof. Dr. Sarah Diefenbach is a leading figure in the field of UX, combining her expertise in Economic Psychology and Human-Computer Interaction with a deep understanding of user experience design. Currently a professor at Ludwig-Maximilians-University of Munich, she has dedicated her career to advancing the integration of psychology and ergonomics into the design of user-centered systems. Her academic journey spans notable roles, from postdoctoral work in User Experience and Ergonomics at Folkwang University of Arts to research assistant positions at the University of Würzburg and the University of Koblenz-Landau.

Recognized for her academic contributions, Sarah Diefenbach has received prestigious accolades, including the Best Paper Award at the Mensch & Computer Conference and the Best Session Award at the Usability Professionals Conference. Her commitment to blending psychological principles with user interface design has shaped her academic work and influenced practical applications across industries, solidifying her status as a Titan in the UX field.

18.16 Thomas Vöhringer-Kuhnt

Dr. Thomas Vöhringer-Kuhnt is a prominent figure in the UX industry. He is known for his extensive experience in the practical application of UX research and development methods and for mentoring the next generation of UX professionals. With leadership roles across several prestigious automotive companies, including Mazda Motor Europe, Geely/Lotus Tech Innovation Centre, and Continental, he has been instrumental in shaping the future of

Human-Machine Interface and user experience in the automotive sector. His expertise in product development, UX design, and leadership has made him a trusted mentor at CareerFoundry, where he guides aspiring UX professionals.

In addition to his corporate and mentoring roles, Thomas Vöhringer-Kuhnt has significantly contributed to the UX community as the host of the "Lead UX - The User Experience Leadership Circle" podcast. His work is driven by a passion for improving user experiences and sharing his knowledge to make products and services more user-friendly and impactful. His deep understanding of the intersection between design, psychology, computer science, and engineering, combined with his leadership in global UX projects, makes him a true Titan in the field of UX.

18.17 Tobias Oberpaul

Tobias Oberpaul is a leading force in the world of UX, demonstrating exceptional leadership and innovation in his role at Deutsche Bahn (DB). With a career rooted in a deep understanding of user experience, Tobias has built a reputation for transforming UX into a strategic asset that drives organizational success.

Currently serving as the Lead of DB UX, Tobias Oberpaul plays a pivotal role in guiding the UX vision for Deutsche Bahn. Under his leadership, DB UX has developed a robust, company-wide UX ecosystem that spans design processes, tools, resources, and education. His leadership oversees the UX Design System, which fosters collaboration between designers and developers, ensuring a consistent and user-centered approach to digital product development. By championing transparency and strategic decision-making through the UX Council, Tobias Oberpaul ensures that UX is woven into DB's innovation and digital transformation.

Tobias Oberpaul's career path reflects his deep commitment to creating impactful digital experiences. Before his work at DB, he co-founded SOVYY, where he and his team continue to shape digital products that push boundaries. His tenure at Techpilot and Fidor Bank also highlights his expertise in design systems, product development, and cross-functional collaboration, contributing to developing cohesive, high-quality digital platforms.

Through his strategic vision, collaborative approach, and commitment to advancing the field of UX, Tobias Oberpaul has established himself as a true Titan in the industry.

18.18 Ulf Schubert

Ulf Schubert is an expert in User Experience and Customer Experience (CX) with over 20 years of experience driving innovation and growth across B2B and software industries. As the Director of UX & Touchpoint Design at DATEV eG, Schubert has played a pivotal role in shaping customer-centric strategies and developing award-winning digital products. His expertise spans UX and CX management, strategy implementation, and the transformation of organizations to become more user-centered and data-driven.

Ulf Schubert's leadership in UX extends to his mentoring role as the founder of the Experience Leadership Club, where he empowers fellow UX and CX professionals to enhance their leadership capabilities. He is a recognized UX expert, accredited by UXPA International, and has successfully led cross-functional teams to foster collaboration and improve user journeys in complex, agile environments.

With a deep commitment to organizational development and a passion for elevating UX maturity, Ulf Schubert excels at guiding businesses through times of change, ensuring they remain agile and responsive to evolving customer needs. His work in UX and CX communities and his focus on leadership development positions him as a true Titan in the field, influencing both the strategic direction of companies and the growth of future UX leaders.

18.19 Uwe Betzin

Uwe Betzin is a prominent figure in the field of UX and is renowned for his innovative approach to integrating design and development processes. With over two decades of experience in software development, Uwe Betzin has evolved from a senior developer to a visionary UX leader, now serving as the Head of UX at generic.de. His extensive software engineering and UX design background makes him a unique catalyst for bridging the gap between the technical and user-centered aspects of product development.

At generic.de, Uwe is committed to shaping enterprise software projects, prioritizing user experience, and using key Dual Track Agile and Clean Code Development principles. His approach emphasizes continuous product discovery and seamless UX integration throughout the software lifecycle, from presales to maintenance. By guiding his team of six UX designers, Uwe fosters an environment where creativity and technical precision flourish, ensuring that software is functional, intuitive, and engaging for end-users.

Before his role at generic.de, Uwe Betzin contributed significantly to SAP, where he designed and optimized user experiences for S/4HANA and played a key role in developing the widely praised "Design Eye Opener" course. His efforts in training and mentoring have reached thousands, helping foster a company-wide UX mindset that elevates every aspect of software development.

Uwe Betzin's passion for UX is grounded in his belief that well-executed software should satisfy all stakeholders – developers, users, and customers. His extensive knowledge of software development, combined with his focus on Agile UX, positions him as a true UX Titan, driving forward-thinking strategies that redefine how enterprise software is created and experienced.

19

About the authors

Chapter nineteen

About the authors

Dr. Benjamin Franz

Benjamin Franz founded the Data-Driven UX Design Agency Custom Interactions in 2013, together with his wife, Michaela. With his background in mechanical engineering and his doctorate in user interface design, he has more than 15 years of experience designing user interfaces that are easy to use and delightful for the user. Besides being the head of a design agency, Benjamin shares his knowledge as an author, lecturer, and speaker and has a knack for software development.

Dr. Michaela Kauer-Franz

Michaela Kauer-Franz is co-founder of Custom Interactions together with her husband Benjamin. Since 2017, she has been head of the business unit Custom Medical. With her background in psychology and her doctorate in acceptance of technology, she has been striving for almost two decades to design devices that matter. Michaela's work is focused on user research and user needs. She shares her knowledge as an author, lecturer, and speaker and is enthusiastic about the soft skills needed for UX success.

www.ingramcontent.com/pod-product-compliance
Lightning Source LLC
Chambersburg PA
CBHW041258210926
51847CB00009B/67
9783000818196